Advance Praise for

THE MYSTERY OF CHILDREN

"An extraordinary book. Mike Mason has shaken me to the core of my soul—he knows me."

Brennan Manning, author of
*Ruthless Trust* and *The Ragamuffin Gospel*

"This joyful, honest, and compelling read calls me to be grateful for every laugh and each tear I have been granted as a parent and a child. Mike is a beautiful writer and a better man because he has heeded the call to listen and to become as a child."

Dan Allender, president of Mars Hill Graduate School, Seattle, Washington, and author of *The Healing Path*

"Mike Mason commends a radical idea—rather than demanding that our kids grow up and act 'like adults,' we grownups need to learn anew the simplicities and glories of childhood for ourselves. Page after page Mason makes observations that are so transparently true we wonder why we never noticed or thought or spoke like that before."

Luci Shaw, writer in residence, Regent College, and author of *The Angles of Light* and *Writing the River*

D1636200

248.8
M

c.1

# The
# MYSTERY
# *of*
# CHILDREN

*What Our Kids Teach Us About Childlike Faith*

# MIKE MASON

WATERBROOK
PRESS

STAUNTON PUBLIC LIBRARY

THE MYSTERY OF CHILDREN
PUBLISHED BY WATERBROOK PRESS
2375 Telstar Drive, Suite 160
Colorado Springs, Colorado 80920
*A division of Random House, Inc.*

Scripture taken from the *Holy Bible, New International Version*®. NIV® Copyright © 1973,
1978, 1984 by International Bible Society. Used by permission of Zondervan Publishing
House. All rights reserved. Lowercase pronouns for deity have been maintained in quotations
from the NIV in observance of copyright law. Scripture quotations marked (KJV) are taken
from the *King James Version.*

ISBN 1-57856-422-0

Copyright © 2001 by Mike Mason

All rights reserved. No part of this book may be reproduced or transmitted in any form or
by any means, electronic or mechanical, including photocopying and recording, or by any
information storage and retrieval system, without permission in writing from the publisher.

WATERBROOK and its deer design logo are registered trademarks of WaterBrook Press,
a division of Random House, Inc.

Library of Congress Cataloging-in-Publication Data
Mason, Mike, 1952-
    The mystery of children : what our kids teach us about childlike faith / Mike Mason.—
1st ed.
        p.  cm.
    Includes bibliographical references.
    ISBN 1-57856-422-0
    1. Parents—Religious life.    2. Parent and child—Religious aspects—Christianity.
I. Title.

BV4529. M365 2001
248.8'45—dc21

                                                            2001017538

Printed in the United States of America
2001—First Edition

10   9   8   7   6   5   4   3   2   1

*for*

HEATHER

*the One and Only*

# Contents

# CONTENTS

# PREFACE

*He took a little child and had him stand among them.*

MARK 9:36

When I mention to people that I've written a book called *The Mystery of Children,* they often react with a dry, rueful laugh and the words, "Yes, they are a mystery, aren't they?" This surprisingly common response tells me that people's feelings about children are somewhat troubled, as mine have been. The reason for this book is to locate the source of this dilemma, not with children but with one particular child: the one who now reads this book.

Years ago I took a course in which the professor outlined the various ages through which the Christian church has passed in its two-thousand-year history. A primary symbol or archetype that dominated the thinking of believers throughout an era could characterize each age. For example, the earliest centuries of the church could be labeled the Age of the Martyr. Later came the Age of the Monk, the Age of the Pilgrim, the Age of the Soldier of Christ, and so on. My professor, Dr. James Houston, concluded this lecture with a statement I have never forgotten: "The age the church is presently passing through is the Age of the Child."

I have no doubt this is true. As the church enters its third millennium, it is no longer sufficient for Christians to set their hearts on being martyrs, pilgrims, or soldiers. It is not enough to be a pastor, an evangelist, a monk, a missionary, a charitable worker, or a writer of devotional books. No, as the cloud of darkness deepens over the earth, and as sin itself grows and mutates to develop ever more complex and sophisticated strains of wickedness, the world is looking for something brand-new.

In its last days the world needs not more Christianity but a new kind of Christianity, a new breed of Christian. If the world is to be renewed one more time, it will be through you and me obeying Christ's call to become like little children. In a sense, it is time for the church herself to be born again.

Is this not the role that children play in the Bible? They are renewers, groundbreakers and world-shakers, bearers of new seed, heralds of a new age. For the world grows old and tired and dies, over and over. It does not have in itself the capacity for renewal or rebirth. Only a fresh touch from God can revive it. This may come in a multitude of ways. But characteristically when God does a brand-new thing, He does it through a child.

And so the Bible is full of children and babies, godly infants who influenced the course of sacred history as profoundly as any adult has. Some people may laugh at this idea, which is why the first of these wondrous children was named Isaac, a word meaning *laugh*. Isaac was the original grace-child, the child of divine promise who simply by being born confounded all reasonable notions of how religion ought to work.

And then there was Moses. Who can doubt that God was just as present, just as deeply engaged in the saving of His people, through the baby Moses as He was through the adult Moses?

Hebrews 11:23 tells us that "by faith Moses' parents hid him for three months after he was born, because they saw he was no ordinary child." What did they see? How could they know that this newborn was not ordinary?

They must have known it the same way the shepherds knew when they entered the stable in Bethlehem, or the way the Magi knew when they set down their costly gifts—including all their lowly adult wisdom—at the feet of a child. They knew by divine revelation.

A child *is* a revelation from God. Prophets receive visions, mystics ponder the ineffable, great preachers deliver God's word. But the greatest revelation comes through flesh and blood. Every child is a fresh, unheard-of image of God, and children keep coming and coming because the world has not yet conceived of all the fullness of God's glory.

If God were a painter, He would paint not with brush and oils but with babies. If God were a historian, He would write the history of the world not with kings and armies but with children. If God were a preacher, He would preach not with words but with you and me, His own dear sons and daughters.

As the New Testament opens, all eyes are upon a child. And what a child this was! In one birth are gathered together all the Old Testament threads of God's saving action through infants. The baby Jesus was the crowning fulfillment of them all, and much more. He was something the world had never seen before, something utterly new: an uncreated person! Every other human being was made by the Creator; this One alone was begotten. Not only was Christ not made, but "through him all things were made." This holy child "was with God in the beginning" and now "the true light that gives light to every man was coming into the world" (John 1:2,3,9).

There is something marvelous and revolutionary about the world's having to orient itself around a child for renewal, about the church's having to look to a child to light its way. Mark Twain commented on how much more fun life would be if we could be born at eighty and gradually work our way back to eighteen. He didn't have the guts to go any further—down to eight, say, or back to one or two. But in the spiritual life, as T. S. Eliot put it, "The way up is the way down, the way forward is the way back."[1] This is the way God Himself took when the Ancient of Days chose to don diapers.

So: Become a good child. Go back to square one, back to the kindergarten of your soul. Revert to the roots of your own childhood and make peace with your beginnings. Rediscover there the secrets of your inmost heart, which are revealed only to little children. Everything you need for your whole life was once freely given to you. Do you remember?

As my earlier book *The Mystery of Marriage* explored the parallels between human marriage and our relationship with God, so *The Mystery of Children* does the same with the parent-child relationship. More than a manual on parenting, this book is for everyone who wishes to become childlike in heart or to be closer to children, and I hope to show that these two goals are intimately entwined. The way to be a good parent is by growing in childlike faith, and the way to become childlike is to love a child.

This book is a patchwork of stories, theological reflections, extracts from a diary I kept as my daughter was growing up, and other various musings. My approach has been deliberately fragmentary—more a journal than a continuous essay or narrative—because those who spend much time with young children tend to lead fragmented lives. With two or three toddlers around, one doesn't sit down to read *War and Peace*. It can be hard enough to find time to read one chapter of the Bible. So I've provided a book of short chapters made up of shorter sections, suitable for digesting at odd moments. This is a rocking chair book, a bathroom book, a car book for the employees of Mom & Dad's Taxi.

The twenty-six chapters each relate roughly to one half-year of a child's life. There is a chapter one, but there is also a chapter one-half and a chapter one and a half. I've even included a chapter zero because that's the age of a baby at birth. With each chapter I invite the reader to enter imaginatively into that age. What is it like relating to a six-and-a-half-year-old? What is it like being one? Are there not times when you still feel three or four in your relationship with God?

The reason for half-chapters should be obvious, for children count their lives not in whole years but by halves. They want everyone to know they are not just six but six and a half. In our family we take this so far that we actually celebrate our daughter's half-birthday, complete with half a birthday cake (no chocolate) and the singing of half the "Happy Birthday" song (either the first two lines or every second syllable: "Ha _ birth _ to _ Ha _" etc.)

Sadly, I had to end my book at chapter twelve and a half. I would have liked to keep going until chapter forty-nine, which is my age as this book goes to press. However, isn't it true that something of childhood gets left behind around the age of twelve? Besides, since my daughter Heather has just turned thirteen, my expertise as a parent does not yet extend to the teenage years (though this did not stop me from ending the book with a few reflections on the terra incognita of adolescence).

Every book has a muse, someone who inspires the writer. Without the inspiration of the muse, the book could never have been written. My muse has been Heather. Rather than writing about childhood in the abstract, I'm writing about one particular child named Heather and about how her love for me, and mine for her, has transformed me by causing me to know and to love another particular child—the one who lives inside me.

The particularity of this story is important. As my daughter has been the catalyst for my own growth in childlikeness, I believe everyone needs a similar relationship. On our own we are nothing; all light shines through relationships. We cannot obey Jesus' word to become childlike without loving an actual child. He or she will be our guide into this forgotten land. We can learn a great deal about ancient Rome by reading books or going to museums, but wouldn't it be far more eye-opening to spend a day, or ten years, with an ancient Roman?

Thank you, Heather, for stepping out of the mists of time to take the hand of a blind, aging man. This is our book, yours and mine, and I trust that this deeply personal story will somehow reflect universal truths about the mystery of all children, young and old.

CHAPTER ZERO

# Birth Pangs of Childlikeness

*To us a child is born.*

<br /><br />Isaiah 9:6

"Keep watch," Jesus said, "because you do not know on what day your Lord will come" (Matthew 24:42). I had a graphic reminder of this truth on the day my wife went into labor. I wasn't ready. It was 6:30 A.M. and I hadn't yet had my morning quiet time. I wouldn't have minded going without breakfast, but having to rush my wife to the hospital before I'd prayed was like leaving the house without pants.

Years later this has become a standard joke in our family. Every time this story is told, I'm reminded, "When Jesus returns you won't be ready for Him because you'll be too busy praying!"

Little did I realize that this terrible sense of unreadiness would continue to haunt me for ten years. The fact was, I had no idea how to be a father. Some men seem to take naturally to fatherhood; I was not one of them. For every inch of ground I've won in this

<br /><br />1

area, I've had to fight, scramble, tear out my hair, die a thousand deaths.

If only I'd known that my daughter herself would teach me all I needed to know. If only I'd understood the obvious truth that I couldn't be a father on my own, but only with the help of a child. I needed a child's love. I needed to love a child and, just as important, I needed to soak up her love for me. I needed to experience firsthand how different is the love of a child, how different it is from everything else in the world, before I could begin to grasp what Jesus meant by saying, "Become like this."

How could I have guessed that the secret of being a good father lay in becoming like my child so that I could touch her heart? Even God the Father followed this course by sending His Son to earth.

Anyone who has anything to do with children must admit, finally, that this is how the game works. It is less about adults guiding children than about letting them guide us. It is about Isaiah 9:6: "To us a child is born...and the government will be on his shoulders."

In God's scheme the government of the world is upon the shoulders of children. For "the kingdom of God belongs to such as these" (Luke 18:16).

I first met my daughter, Heather Lynne Mason, on the morning of March 28, 1987. Catching my first glimpse of her was like seeing an angel. I'm not exaggerating; this is literally how I felt.

What I saw was an oval shape not much bigger than the number "0" on this page. This was the top of my daughter's head as it first appeared coming out of her mother's body. A hairy, mucky smear is all it was—yet to me it was a glimpse of another world, a wholly other reality. I had known about this other world for some nine months, but so far it had remained invisible.

Now, suddenly, here it was! I was setting my eyes upon a visitor from another planet.

As the head emerged and grew bigger, it took on roundedness. Now the experience was like being an astronaut in outer space and seeing those first awesome views of the earth's curvature. I gaped in wonder.

Meanwhile, luckily, my wife was pushing like a trooper, and soon the whole little angel popped out and was in our arms, screaming bloody murder. I remember cutting the cord and being surprised at how meaty it was.

The time was 1:03 A.M. on a Saturday. A few minutes later, as I gazed into those inscrutable, light-drenched, newborn eyes, I could almost swear they opened like little mouths and spoke words. They said, "My name is Heather."

This came as a surprise. Beforehand we hadn't been able to decide on a name, but now we knew; she told us herself. And ever since then Heather has been telling us who she is.

Later that night, until dawn, I sat at a long table in the hospital cafeteria and spilled onto paper all the thoughts that were crowding my mind about the birth of my first child. It was a time of stupendous revelation, of the opening of heaven. Just before leaving

Karen and Heather that night, I had read aloud the Christmas story from Luke. Though it was nowhere near Christmas, with our little family nestled together in the birthing bed, our hearts so full, I sensed intuitively how God must have spoken to Mary and Joseph and the shepherds, telling them great and wonderful things they did not know.

I still have those dazzling pages that I wrote in the first hours of Heather's life. They're contained in a blue binder I have open before me right now. To quote just a few lines:

> Heather is so wise! She seems to have come to us from so far away—and yet from so near too, only a few layers of tissue away. Truly "the kingdom of God is within you" (Luke 17:21).

A new baby is a messenger from God. The ultimate divine message arrived in the form of the baby Jesus. "There is nothing new under the sun," groaned the writer of Ecclesiastes (1:9), but the incarnation of God as a human being was something brand-new, a one-and-only event in world history. Yet isn't there a sense in which every new baby reflects the unique glory of that first Christmas? Isn't every birth attended by angels? Doesn't every child arrive directly from heaven wrapped in the light of God?

To be sure, the baby Jesus was perfectly pure and innocent, while all other babies are "sinful at birth" (Psalm 51:5). Still, what adult does not sense the peculiar quality of innocence in a baby? A baby is fallen and sinful, but she is also more innocent than her parents. Isn't this because babies have been with God more recently than we have? They have just come from beholding His face.

My wife Karen is a family doctor who has delivered many babies. I've never yet seen her return from a birth without a heavenly glow upon her face. No matter how tired and spent she may be, no matter at what wee hour the wee one has arrived, no matter how long and arduous the birth process, Karen nevertheless appears bathed in the warmth of an otherworldly light and energy. It's as if she has stood in the doorway of heaven, poked her own head through, and been drenched with celestial radiance.

A similar phenomenon can often be observed at death. The veil parts and a windy light blows through from the other world. Sometimes angels or heavenly scenes are glimpsed. Whereas death is a parting, birth is a welcoming. At a birth not only does the doorway to heaven swing open, but a physical package arrives from there. When my wife returns from the hospital, she seems not only to have caught a glimpse of heaven, but to have reached out and touched that vision. Flushed with happiness, like John she cannot contain the news of that "which we have heard, which we have seen with our eyes, which we have looked at and our hands have touched" (1 John 1:1).

I felt just this way at Heather's birth. Holding divine mystery in my arms, I knew without doubt that this child had more to teach us than we could ever teach her. For she knew more! Somehow she knew more of the important things. As Heather's parents, we knew about life on earth and would train her in its ways. But she knew about the life of heaven, for she had just come from there.

Another comment I wrote on the night of Heather's birth reads:

> When Karen and I were engaged we'd sit up half the night just
> gazing at each other and babbling. There was so much getting
> to know to do! And now this same phenomenon is happening
> with tiny Heather.

Little did I realize how prophetic these words would prove to be of our lifestyle over the next couple of years. Having a baby would indeed put a whole new spin on the word *nightlife*. That first night, however, it was no trouble to stay up till all hours, so bathed in bliss we were. It was like falling in love all over again.

The first three days of Heather's life I stayed in a guest wing of the hospital, which happened to be on Heather Street. On the second morning, a Sunday, I went to church in the hospital chapel.

There were three of us in the congregation. We were led by two others, a man and a woman who were among the dreariest-looking servants of the Lord I have ever met. I'm sure they were good souls, but they were tired—very, very tired. Bone-weary people who keep on doggedly doing their duty take on a faded look, like lampshades badly in need of dusting.

So the faded woman played a faded organ and the faded man

preached a faded sermon and we all read some faded prayers out of a faded book. Nevertheless, for me there was no lack of glory in that service, for the whole time my heart blazed like a star, melting in wonder and shooting off fiery streams of thankfulness and praise.

Why? Because I had just become a father! Because a new baby—my own!—had been born into the world! Is this not the essence of the good news? Unto us a child is born! Oh, sing and celebrate! Clasp hands with the sun and dance a merry jig! On that day nothing and no one could rob me of joy.

In this way, from the very beginning my tiny daughter began to teach me the mysteries of childlikeness. For that morning in the hospital chapel I learned a great lesson about church. I learned that it matters not a whit whether the pastor is a dusty old lampshade, whether the organ sounds like an asthmatic bullfrog, or whether the congregation has three or three thousand. All that matters is that my own heart be soft and open and full of praise.

Those first few days with Heather in the hospital were all like that, pure bliss. Of course during this time I didn't have to do anything with my baby except visit her. Nestling into the hospital bed beside my wife, I'd pull up my shirt and set Heather on my bare tummy for some "bonding" time. What sheer ecstasy this was! Skin-to-skin with my own flesh and blood, I felt in touch with the eternal. However, if the eternal happened to do something unpleasant, I could always just hand her back to Karen. And if things got really rough, I could quietly excuse myself with, "Well, I guess I'll leave you two alone now…"

Yes, for three days I rode a continual high, but the day we

brought our brand-new baby home from the hospital, my bliss was shattered. It happened in one instant. Someone had given Heather a helium balloon, and as we loaded up the car in the parking lot, somehow the balloon got loose and sailed off into the blue.

From that point on, everything went downhill. My mother-in-law was with us, planning to stay for two weeks, and for some reason I blamed the lost balloon on her (though really it was my fault). For the rest of the drive home, over two hours, Karen and her mother chattered away happily, while I gripped the steering wheel and smoldered.

In this black mood I entered the driveway of my baby daughter's first home and hung back as Karen carried her over the threshold, as Karen showed her the river in our backyard and the mountain out the front window, as Karen brought her for the first time into her very own nursery, complete with crib, musical mobile, plush toys, and rocking chair.

All this was lost on me. I lost one of the most special days of my life because I was pouting over a balloon. And thus I discovered one of the first laws of parenting: Those who refuse to become childlike are doomed to be childish.

Of course there was more to my pain than just a lost balloon. I had a list of other gripes and annoyances with the three women in my life. At bottom, I think, I felt left out. There was Grandma and Karen and Heather on one side, and me on the other. I was used to dealing with just one woman. Now I suddenly had three on my hands.

For the next two weeks I felt shoved into the shadows. With

two mothers present, the father had nothing to do. All the feeding, all the cuddling, all the changing of diapers—the mothers looked after everything. I felt like a ten-year-old boy all dressed for his big hockey game but abandoned to sit it out on the bench.

How interesting that, once again, being confronted with a child was bringing up childish feelings in me. Gradually I would learn that this—being plunged back into the unresolved feelings of our own childhood—is precisely our opportunity to grow into child-likeness. For in childhood too I'd been swamped with females. I grew up on a street with a dozen girls but not one boy my own age.

Now, somewhere in my own home, I knew there was a tiny baby, a beautiful, mysterious being, my only child. But so many women were hovering around her that I couldn't get near, so many priestesses murmuring chants, performing strange rituals, whispering to one another and smiling enigmatically. It was as if the Louvre had called and asked me to take care of the *Mona Lisa* for a few days. How marvelous! But when the treasure arrives, it's draped, crated, and hermetically sealed in a steel case.

"Oh no, you mustn't look at it," smiles the curator, simperingly. "Even one glimpse would be quite out of the question."

It was bewildering, enraging, preposterously unfair. However, I could do nothing about it. I was stuck, marooned in a matriarchy.

I know now that all this was my own fault. If it wasn't problems with females, something else would have put my nose out of joint. For the real issue was my own insecurity, my own terrifying sense of inadequacy as a father.

Was I really so keen to get baptized in baby poo? No, because when Karen's mother returned home and I finally got my chance to change a diaper, give a bath, walk the floor at night, all too soon the romanticism of these tasks paled. Looking after the *Mona Lisa* didn't seem nearly so fascinating anymore. I began to wonder when the Louvre might come around to take her back.

As I recall the way my heart sank when I watched Heather's helium balloon sail off into the blue, it strikes me that this event, small in itself, symbolized something larger that got away from me that day. What got away was my sense of control—both control over myself and over the new life that had taken up residence in my home. I would never be able to control Heather, and sensing this made me frightened and furious inside.

One evening around this time I was sitting with Heather in the living room. She had fallen asleep in my lap and I was enjoying an unexpected interlude of peace.

All at once the peace deepened, became somehow radiant, and I felt that Jesus was standing in the center of the room. Though I didn't "see" Him, in a sense I did, for I knew He was there. Similarly, though I did not hear Him say any words, still I received a message. The message was that the child I was holding belonged to Him.

In that moment I thanked the Lord with all my heart for His Heather and gave her back to Him. Prior to this Karen and I had prayerfully dedicated our daughter to the Lord. But this was different. This time it was the Lord's initiative, and a transaction took place that I still do not fully comprehend. All I knew was that I need not worry about this child or about how to look after her, for she belonged to God.

This experience evoked in me a profound sense of relief. It was like standing in the hospital parking lot and watching the helium balloon sail away yet this time just letting it go. With Jesus right there in the room, I tasted the delicious sensation of releasing all control of my daughter. Did this stop me from ever again worrying about Heather or about myself as her father? No. Soon afterward I forgot this incident and I've kept on forgetting it. I would forget it for months, for years at a time. The most difficult part of the Christian faith is remembering.

Many people would like to be prophetic and be able to see into the future. But when it comes to the lessons of God, most of us cannot even see into the past. We forget so quickly. From one day to the next we fail to remember what the Lord has said, what He has done for us, even the most basic facts of the gospel. We are like old people with Alzheimer's. Overnight we can forget that God even exists, and in the morning we must get to know Him all over again.

I am convinced that God speaks regularly to all parents about their children. He is the Father of all, constantly guiding, comforting, reassuring. Those who have ears to hear will hear Him. But will those who have memories remember? It is wonderful to hear the Lord's voice. But who will remember what He has said about our children a week, a month, or ten years later?

Being childlike involves mastering the art, not just of remembering, but of keeping the past so fresh that it seems to be one with the present. Children have no past. For them there are no "good old days"; there are only good new days. When things have always been this way, there is nothing to which to compare the present. There is no past, there is only now. And "now is the time of God's favor, now is the day of salvation" (2 Corinthians 6:2).

Throughout Heather's life I've experienced countless special moments of bonding with her. But for the first ten years my heart was like a sieve, because I failed to keep these experiences fresh. In the midst of the doldrums of parenthood, I'd be paralyzed by the fear that my daughter would grow up to be alienated from her parents, just as I had been. As a child I'd enjoyed many happy times with my parents, but this didn't stop me from putting them through all kinds of grief when I got older. What, then, was the use of trying to build a lasting relationship with Heather? Children, I could testify from firsthand experience, were treacherous and not to be trusted.

Naturally I failed to grasp the tragic irony of this conclusion. I did not see that the corollary of not trusting Heather was that I did not trust myself. Since I experienced myself, at a deep level, as a treacherous child, how could I be anything except a treacherous adult and father?

If only I had understood that being a father is not something I needed to become but something I already *was*. It's like being pregnant: Either you are or you aren't. There's no middle ground. Over time I could grow in maturity as a father, but I would never be *more* of a father than I was at the outset. Even becoming a maturer father, like becoming a maturer Christian, happens only by realizing who I am already, realizing the nature of the relationship I am already in and accepting it more profoundly.

It's the same with childlikeness. We become children simply by being born, not by obedience to a family's rules. Moreover, once we are children we never stop being children, just as once we are parents we never stop being parents. Childhood and parenthood have this in common: They are lifetime vocations.

The lifetime vocation of childhood may seem a strange concept to adults, but isn't this what Christianity is really about? Jesus wants us to know that through faith in Him we are children of our heavenly Father, and that this has always been our true identity. Children are our bridge into this mystery. They are our guides—indeed our parents!—in the realm of childlikeness.

The night I held my sleeping daughter on my lap and Jesus came into the room and claimed her as His own, I became like a child myself, resting in my heavenly Father's arms. Being childlike with Him, it turned out, was all I needed to be a father.

# THE CRY OF THE HEART

*Out of the depths I cry to you, O LORD;*
*O Lord, hear my voice.*

PSALM 130:1-2

All babies cry. I've heard about placid babies, but only the way I've heard about other mythical creatures like gryphons and basilisks. Dogs bark, cats meow, crows caw, and babies cry and go goo-goo. Wails and gurgles are their natural language. It's what they're supposed to say.

A verse in a Christmas carol goes,

The cattle are lowing, the baby awakes,
But little Lord Jesus—no crying He makes.

I don't believe this for a minute. Jesus cried as an adult—why not as a child? And He didn't just cry out of compassion or sorrow; He also cried tears of frustration and desperate, naked need: "During the days of Jesus' life on earth, he offered up prayers and petitions with loud cries and tears to the one who could save him from death" (Hebrews 5:7).

Isn't there something we adults stand to learn from our children's tears? Becoming childlike is painful. Growing up is painful; growing down is even more so because we are more conscious of the process. No step in this backward direction can be taken without our cooperation. We never asked to grow up, but we must ask to grow down. We must cry out to the One who can help us.

Who better to learn crying from than a baby? Babies are little soldiers—infantry (excuse the pun) whose unswerving mission is to scale their parents' walls, invade their inner sanctum and knock down all their cherished defenses against pure, irrational feelings.

No, parents, you are not paranoid. Babies really have been sent into your life to confuse all your plans, to frustrate your best intentions, to outwit you at every turn and to drive you to your knees.

In short: to reduce you to tears, just like themselves.

For you are exactly the same, you two. One's big, one's little, but there the difference ends, and God would have you know this. He wants you to know that you too are but a mewling little rosebud, kicking in your blankets and screaming bloody murder whenever the big Butler-in-the-Sky doesn't bring your food and drink on a silver platter at precisely the right time.

God, our parent, wants us to know this not just in theory but in our existential gut. He wants us to feel this truth in the very marrow of our bones. Because when we do—when we finally give up on being a Big Person and acquiesce to being only a Little

Person—we might just relax enough to stop being a control freak and to receive into our soul the peace that passes understanding.

Strange and wonderful things happen at odd hours of the night when you're up with a crying child.

One morning toward dawn, at her wits' end after a long vigil, Karen finally roused me. "To you I throw the torch," she announced, passing me the kid and almost immediately falling asleep.

Unable to comfort Heather, I carried her out to the living room and sat her on the top edge of the couch. I often did this so she could look out the big picture window. We had a beautiful view into a yard filled with flowers and trees and in the near distance a snowcapped mountain adorned with a waterfall. In the dawn light this scene appeared ravishingly soft and magical, like a Renaissance painting.

Yet all this wasn't enough to stop Heather from crying and fussing and squirming like a piglet, and I was just about to give up when something happened. Something stupendous.

Suddenly, out of the very mouth of the dawn, appeared two enormous Canada geese. They seemed to come from nowhere. At the moment we saw them, they were but a house-length away, and before we could breathe they were upon us. They flew low, heart-stoppingly low, and flat-out straight toward us with all their magnificent power. I thought for sure they would crash right through our window, but at the last moment they veered upward and soared out of sight just above the roofline.

How gigantic they were! Zooming in like that out of the blue, they were like apparitions, or like something primal, prehistoric, from the dawn of time. Of course I'd seen Canada geese before, lots of them, and at closer range. They breed like dandelions around here.

But it was the setting: first light of day, the time-between-times, nothing stirring, the world outside like a dream, me still half-asleep and Heather crying like breaking glass—and then all at once these colossal flying animals looming like jet planes.

"LOOK!" I yelled to Heather, pointing dazedly, and tiny infant though she was, I knew she really saw them. For immediately she stopped crying, went dead still, and together we caught our breaths as the prodigies cleared our eyeballs by mere feet. And then we sat like statues, the two of us, gazing out in quiet wonder at a brand-new morning transformed, hallowed, by this wondrous portent of the geese.

Heather's little face grew suddenly so solemn, so awed. At least, I interpreted it as awe. It's hard to know for sure because three minutes later she was sound asleep.

I've never forgotten those geese. In that peculiar ambiance of mood and setting, they were like no other geese I had ever seen. Potent, magical, world-shattering. So close I could almost count their feathers. And clearly bearing news, on swift and powerful wings, of the majesty of God.

Just think: If Heather hadn't been having a fussy night, I would never have seen this. In those few moments she and I were one, the same age, or no age at all. She stopped her fussing, and I stopped mine, and I went back to bed thinking: One morning we shall wake up and the whole world will be like those geese. Nothing anymore will be "just ordinary" for "the earth will be full of the knowledge of the LORD as the waters cover the sea" (Isaiah 11:9).

Someday I'd like to write a book called *One Thousand Ways to Stop a Baby from Crying, All of Which Work Only Once.*

When the technique that works is always the last one you try, and when the same technique doesn't work the next time, you begin to suspect that the time it did work might have been an accident. Babies love to play this game, and it has certain rules, such as: The more important it is for a certain technique to work, the less likely will baby cooperate.

One technique that worked well with Heather was the mechanical swing. When you put the kid in this contraption and wound the spring, it went back and forth for about five minutes, making the most horrible clacking noise. But at least the baby was quiet.

I loved the mechanical swing because it worked when nothing else did, but I also hated it. It offended my aesthetics. I was a purist who believed in natural methods like rocking chairs and human arms. But no, Heather had to be a child of the machine age. I know now that she did this out of spite. I know because thirteen years later she's still doing it, still deliberately embracing views that are diametrically opposed to mine, just to keep me on my toes.

Isn't it interesting how when a baby is crying, all your lovely aesthetics go out the window? Suddenly you become keenly focused not on what is lovely, or true, or admirable, but simply on what works. Short of hauling out the sledgehammer, whatever works to shut that little valve on a kid's throat, you do it.

What would happen if we ran our lives this way? What if we took the crying of our own souls seriously enough to insist on doing only what works? What if we became urgently committed to bringing comfort to our deepest, heartfelt cries and following at all costs the way of peace? Maybe then our souls, knowing that we are really and truly there for them, would gradually outgrow their noisiness and surprise us with their quiet nature. Maybe in time our own hearts would come to trust us, and we them.

Crying babies, though we are loath to admit it, remind us all too readily of ourselves. Don't our needs match theirs in intensity? The only difference is that as adults we tend to keep our mouths shut and scream in quieter ways: worry, control, blame, despair.

Our soul is like a baby because we do not know when it will sleep or when it will wake, when it will be content or when it will seem to work against us, when it will demand attention or require a change. Like our soul a baby hasn't got much flesh. It doesn't yet know how to hide in the folds of the flesh, and so whatever it feels inside is immediately registered shamelessly on the surface.

When children wail, we adults feel insecure. This is why we are desperate to shut them up. Babies know nothing of politeness or decorum. They have no respect for social custom, no common decency. They make no effort to censor their thoughts; they simply open their mouths and speak loudly exactly what is on their minds: WAAAAAAAAAAAHHHHHHHHHHHHHH!!!

The crying of children testifies to the untamed presence of darkness in our world and may remind us that we have forgotten how to cry about this ourselves. In a repressed society, babies have the important job of candidly expressing emotion for everyone else. While the rest of us stoically bury our noisier feelings in vaults of concrete, babies do the crying for the whole world.

When Joshua and the Israelites overthrew the city of Jericho, their chief weapon was noise. Every day for a week the people marched once around the city, led by seven priests blowing seven trumpets. On the seventh day the trumpets blared and the people gave a great shout and the walls of the city crumbled. So effective was this strategy that, according to Revelation 8–9, the Lord plans to use it again at the end of time when seven trumpets will initiate seven stages of the world's destruction.

I wonder if God had something similar in mind when He issued infants with such robust lungs? Surely the crying of children, day after day, night after night, is a potent weapon in the destruction of the high-walled, pagan urbanity of adulthood. Slowly the whole world as one knew it wobbles, shifts, and finally crumbles to pieces before the onslaught of these incessant, high-pitched cries.

In the long run, we can do nothing except throw in our lot with the children. Indeed we must return to our own childhood and there recover the cries, the screams, the babbles, and coos of that little person inside who reacts unthinkingly to the overwhelming immediacy of raw life in all of its dazzling enormity.

I well remember the day I recovered my primal scream. Until then I'd coped pretty well with caring for my daughter in the afternoons while Karen was at work. But gradually Heather's increased mobility began to catch up with me.

I was trying so hard, so heroically, to be the perfect dad. The idea of admitting, coolly and sensibly, that something wasn't working, that possibly something had to change—this thought was far too threatening. All my fatherly instincts clamored to stifle any hint that I might be failing at my task.

Nevertheless, I couldn't go on. The fine, thick walls of my sanity were crumbling. Until finally one day the screaming blue meany inside of me popped out of his box.

Heather was doing something naughty—who knows what? All I remember is that I threw myself down on the floor, pounded my fists on the carpet and screamed. I recall exactly what I yelled. It was something like, "Ahhhhhhhhhhhhhhhhhhhhh!!!" followed by, "God, get me out of this!" over and over.

My first yells, I think, were choked and pitiful, like someone barely alive stirring inside a coffin. But even this felt so good that I soon got the hang of it and cut loose. The fist pounding was especially therapeutic. People yell at hockey games, but society needs more volunteers to lie prostrate on their own living room floors and beat the daylights out of their carpets.

I don't know what Heather thought of this. I didn't stop to notice. I wasn't thinking of her at all. For a few blessed moments in that long, grueling afternoon of childcare, my one thought was for myself. How wonderful this felt! When it was all over, I had a beautiful sensation of lightness and peace, like the sun coming out after a thunderstorm.

That evening Karen and I sat down to explore options. Before this I couldn't have seen, could not even have contemplated, any way out. Now I knew there *had* to be a way out.

As it happened, there was a family down the street, friends from our church, who would be happy to take Heather for a couple of hours each afternoon. They had three kids, a dog, swings, a tree house—a perfect setup for Heather. She needed out of the box as much as I did.

So we arranged for our tiny girl to go out into the big world each day, almost as if she were heading off to work and leaving little Daddy at home to play on his computer. This arrangement worked beautifully for the next few years, until Heather was ready to attend preschool.

Still, I can't help wondering about that meltdown of mine on the living room floor. It certainly worked; it got me what I wanted. However, adults cannot scream and pound every time our wants are frustrated…can we?

Perhaps not. Yet adult cries, just like a baby's, signal time for a change. In this case, what would have happened if, instead of farming out my kid, I'd made a different change? What if, instead of behaving like a child, I'd become one? What if I'd gotten down on the floor not to pound and yell but to play? Or what if I'd let my daughter's tears do what they are ultimately meant to do, which is teach compassion?

Oddly enough, after so many years of Heather's noisy lungs, I have only one clear memory of a time when I actually heard her crying. She was older by then, maybe as old as nine. I have no idea what she was crying about; all I recall is the sound and what it did to me.

I was in my room and she was in hers, at the other end of the hall. I was trying to think what to do about whatever her problem was, when all at once, instead of trying to shut out the distraction so I could think, I actually heard the sound of my daughter's crying. To my surprise, it wasn't the grating, raucous cacophony I'd always taken it for. Instead it was soft, plaintive, deeply touching, and compelling. I was so moved that I went straight to her room and knew instinctively how to comfort her.

After this, I noticed, her tearful outbursts grew less frequent, reserved for real shocks and wounds and largely purged of manipulation.

Heather's crying, it seemed, had served its purpose. After nine years someone finally got the message. Her father finally heard her.

# WORDS AND THINGS

*At that time Jesus, full of joy through the Holy Spirit, said,*
*"I praise you, Father, Lord of heaven and earth,*
*because you have hidden these things from the wise and learned,*
*and revealed them to little children.*
*Yes, Father, for this was your good pleasure."*

LUKE 10:21

First things, then words. First we discover things, then we discover words for the things. At least this is how it works with humans. With God it's the opposite. "In the beginning was the Word" (John 1:1). First He spoke, then the things came into being.

I wonder: Before anything was made, was anything said? Did God speak before creation? Apparently as the Spirit of God brooded over the waters, all was silence. When He did speak, what language did He use? If every word of His gave rise to a new creation, could His language be called the language of things? Are His words stars and oceans and tigers?

It's an October afternoon and Heather is seven months old. She's sitting on the living room floor in a pool of autumn sunlight stained red-gold by the blazing maple tree in our front yard. If I knew anything about psychology (which I don't), I would call this the object-oriented phase of child development. For the last fifteen minutes Heather has been absorbed in investigating a yellow plastic ball.

Any adult can tell you that a ball looks much the same no matter which side you look at. But Heather has been turning that ball around and around, examining it from every conceivable angle, just as if she were a Renaissance explorer circumnavigating the globe and discovering untold wonders. Or maybe to her (who knows?) the real wonder is that the ball is exactly the same all the way around. Maybe I am witnessing Heather Mason's discovery of Round.

Don't let anyone tell you that children have short attention spans. Like adults, they have short attention spans for things that don't interest them. But for things that intrigue them, their concentration is wonderful to behold. Heather's absorption, so rapt and serene, has a kind of sanctifying effect upon everything she touches. At this stage ribbons and strings are her favorites, perhaps because of the particularly fine motor skills required for handling them.

A baby's fascination with objects is literally consuming, since everything has to undergo the oral test. A baby takes the world into herself one bite at a time. How beautiful to watch a human being passionately in love, even infatuated, with the intricacy of the physical world! Of course it is not for its own sake that the world should be loved, but for what it tells us about the Creator, the One who made it.

This is exactly what babies excel at. They aren't into material possessions. They do not prize the things themselves so much as what can be learned from them. Unless something is right in their hands, they probably don't even remember it exists, let alone pine for it. What they retain is the spiritual essence of the thing. The yellow ball itself Heather casts aside, but its satisfying weight, its softness, the intensity of its color—these qualities remain with her.

If what infants do with things qualifies as "thinking," what exactly do they think about? I suggest they don't just ask What is this thing? and How does it work? but Where did it come from? To them it is an object from another world. Babies don't compute that they are in that other world right now; they are too newly arrived. So every new object is like a rock from Pluto. A rock, in itself, has little meaning. What matters is: What can it tell me about the other world?

For an adult the information encoded in a yellow ball concerns no "other world," only this world. But for infants every object speaks of another world, and that other world is Paradise, the only world for which they were created. Children remind us that the physical world is the kindergarten of the soul. They don't artificially divide the physical and spiritual. The sky is the color of God's eyes, the stars are the twinkles in them, and clouds are the crinkles at their corners.

Children hallow small things. A child is a priest of the ordinary, fulfilling a sacred office that absolutely no one else can fill. The simplest gesture, the ephemeral moment, the commonest object all become precious beyond words when touched, noticed, lived by one's own dear child.

Just to watch a child at this work of exploring every detail of some perfectly ordinary physical object—this is an act of contemplation, which itself has a sanctifying effect upon the observer. After Heather has finished with a ball or a ribbon, I'll often pick it up myself and try to see what she saw in it.

I'm reminded of the period after I first became a Christian, when the physical world took on an intense fascination for me. After all, I had new eyes with which to see it. Shapes, colors, textures, the simplest objects—a leaf, a cup, a raindrop—everything seemed to shine with a holy glow, as if somehow both brand-new and more ancient than the universe. If I'd been a painter I would have gone wild. But I didn't go wild; instead the scales crept slowly back over my eyes until I was captured again by the shadowy mundane.

Now I need a child to teach me once more how magical the world is, how everything that exists is charged with an overpowering enchantment, as if some very great artist had just moments before finished making it and departed from the room.

Heather is sitting on the living room floor, whining and complaining. I'm trying to concentrate on reading a book. A sea of toys surrounds her, but nothing satisfies.

Finally I put down my book and lift Heather onto my lap. Quite suddenly she calms down. I find her a toy and for the next twenty minutes she plays with that one toy with rapt attention.

How fascinating! Alone on the floor, all the toys in the world couldn't amuse her. But on Daddy's lap one toy is utterly wonderful.

"Look, Daddy!" she seems to be saying. "What I do is important too!" And it is. It is deeper than the book I've been reading. It's as important as anything an adult does and as worthy of notice. It's the study of physics, chemistry, aesthetics, and everything else. Shouldn't a baby's investigations be published in scholarly journals alongside the work of the Nobel laureates?

While Heather was down on the floor complaining, I'd been feeling frustrated, vaguely dull, distant from God, resentful of being a father. It occurred to me that my relationship with my daughter had become less a matter of love than of business—changing diapers, feeding, wiping up, carting around. While I did my best to make the work fun, there was so much work that I left little place for fun alone.

And I wondered why I felt dull! The moment I took Heather onto my lap, the fog began to melt and a ray of joy penetrated. Why, I wondered, do I expect to have my heavenly Father's whole-hearted attention and approval while withholding this same gift from my daughter?

The exterior lives of children present graphic parables of the inner lives of adults. A book of the spiritual lessons I learned in Heather's second year might be entitled *Problems of the Teething Parent*. It is almost as if children playact little dramas of the adult soul. A boy plays with soldiers the way a man does business. A child learns to talk the way we all learn to pray. A baby plays with a balloon the way an adult explores inner freedom: trying out what it feels like, seeing how it works, testing what brings it close and what drives it away.

One day Heather was playing with a rubber toy that squeaked when squeezed. The only trouble was, without knowing it she kept covering up the squeaker hole with her thumbs, so that no matter how hard she squeezed she couldn't get a sound out of it. This problem so exasperated her that it eventually drove her to tears.

Jumping up and running to her I cried, "Heather, Heather— what's the point of playing with something if it's only going to…"

In midsentence I caught myself. Arrested by a shock of recognition, my voice trailed off as I finished, "to frustrate you?"

I caught myself because that very day I'd behaved exactly like Heather—not with a rubber toy but with a plastic-and-metal one: my new computer. How I got my thumbs over the thing's squeaker hole, I have no idea, but I definitely played with my toy to the point of distraction and far beyond.

Another time, when Heather was about two, she hit one of her friends and made her cry. I punished her by taking away her favorite doll, Baby Blue Eyes, for one day. When the day was half over Heather asked me once, gingerly, if she could have her doll back. There wasn't much life or hope in her asking. She knew when her father was implacable. More importantly, she knew she'd done wrong.

Nevertheless I found myself intensely excited about the moment when I would be able to give Baby Blue Eyes back to Heather. I wished I could hasten that moment, but I could not. The time had been fixed.

Just so, I imagine, our heavenly Father holds Himself in a hushed ecstasy of waiting until the day when all that we sinners have lost in this sorry world through our own and others' folly can be fully restored to us by His own hand. I bet He can hardly wait to see our faces!

First things, then words.

At age one Heather went through a phase of being enchanted with books, paper and print—not as vehicles of language, but merely as objects.

One Sunday at church she spent the entire worship time paging through the hymnal as we sang. She didn't want the book left open at the right hymn. No, she just wanted to turn over one page after another, as if intrigued by the mechanical workings of this strange object we call a book. As if searching out some secret or clue to its operation.

At the same time she seemed absorbed in the sound of the singing. Seeking to divine her thoughts, suddenly I realized: She thinks this beautiful sound emerges somehow from the pages of this book! In a sense, she was right. Just so, as the world examines the lives of Christians, it should become apparent that whatever is good or true or beautiful in such lives is rooted in the pages of a mystical, singing Book.

Around this same time Heather was experimenting with the noises of prelanguage. I recall listening with fascination as she sounded out every consonant and every vowel known to man, including all the non-English ones. Out of her mouth would tumble Chinese nasals, German gutterals, Zulu clicks, and (for all I knew) whole sentences of perfect ancient Hebrew. I seriously wondered whether this chatter might possibly be a language in its own right. Could the angels understand it? Would that make it a form of tongues?

I once heard it proposed that the gobbledygook of infants may be the very language given to Adam and Eve in the Garden of Eden: the language used at their first meeting; the language in which Eve conversed with the serpent; the language that finally was confounded beyond retrieval at the Tower of Babel, but that one day will be gloriously restored to us.

A preposterous thought, no doubt. But when all is revealed about the beginning and the end of things—what secrets we shall know!

Heather's first word, I'm proud to say, was *Dada*. Beyond that I didn't keep any record. But once she started, the words came pouring out. By age three she was a regular motor-mouth, reveling in rambling chains of monologue long on repetition but short on coherence. No doubt verbal diarrhea is an important phase in the development of language, yet how tiresome it can be for listeners.

This led me to wonder: Was my prayer life like this? Did I soliloquize rather than pray? While others prayed in a group, why was I so busy composing? I could hardly wait for others to stop so that I could indulge in my own long-winded ramble! I began to see that even when alone with God, with my mouth closed, I was a "motor-mind." Surely God must heave a big sigh of relief each night, just as I did with Heather, when finally I switched off and went to sleep.

Yet it was also perfectly clear to me that, however much Heather shot off her mouth, God loved her just as dearly. Maybe the essence of spirituality had less to do with ascetic self-discipline than with freedom of expression. Maybe I could relax more about my racing thoughts and tongue and just let myself be loved.

Before Heather learned to talk, I used to wonder what she would say once she got going. What would it be like to have a normal, real conversation with my daughter? What would she tell us about herself? About us? Maybe she'd have messages for us from heaven...

In some ways, after thirteen years, I'm still wondering what sort of thoughts are tumbling around inside my child's brain. Sure, we have great talks now, and they get better and better. But as the talk draws close to the bone in some areas, the point comes when Heather snaps all the blinds shut and suddenly there's no one home. This is a child's prerogative: No, I'm not letting you into that room. Not right now. You want to know me? Figure it out for yourself.

In this way, isn't dialogue with a child a bit like prayer? While we can discover some secrets, there remains much we cannot know.

Certain ways of asking work better than others, and timing is all-important. Therefore abandon pride and all mere inquisitiveness. The indirect, nonchalant approach works best. When talking to children, or to God, don't pry. Certain things may be best left unspoken. Because once the cat's out of the bag there's no getting it back in. For example, how badly do you want to know that your child thinks you're a stuffed shirt?

I no longer wonder what Heather will say when she learns how to talk. Now I know. I've listened to hours and hours of her conversation, years of it.

I know now that she would grow up to say, "Daddy, what are those brown stains on your teeth?"

She would say, "When I get bigger, I want to go and live on Mars."

She would ask me, "Daddy, why do you spend so much time at such a useless job?"

As a teenager she would observe, "Isn't it amazing how well I've turned out without any parental guidance?"

She would casually comment, "Dad, if I were Mommy, I would never have married you. I wouldn't have been that desperate."

No saying of hers, however, would ever stun me more than this one at three years old: "Daddy, you don't love me."

Ouch! What if God were to say this? "Mike, you don't really love Me."

Or how about, "Mike, what are those brown stains on your soul?"

We think we want to hear God's voice. We wonder what He might say to us. But I wasn't joking about the possibility of our children bringing us messages from heaven. They're going to bring us revelations, no doubt about that.

How much do we really want to know?

# WELCOME TO TODDLERHOOD

*Let the little children come to me, and do not hinder them,*
*for the kingdom of God belongs to such as these.*

LUKE 18:16

The second year of life begins with the staggering (literally) advancement of learning to walk. One small step for the babe; one giant setback for Mom and Dad.

Before Heather learned this trick, I'd done the walking for her. At the time I failed to appreciate what a good arrangement this was, for it meant I retained a measure of control. Heather napped for two hours every afternoon, and while she slept I got my writing done. As you will understand, I desperately needed a surefire method of getting her settled down for her nap. For a long time this method was to strap her to my chest in a cloth baby carrier and take her for a walk.

We lived on a quiet crescent, an oval loop with a park in the middle. The loop was a quarter mile long, so it took about fifteen minutes to walk around it once.

On a good day, Heather fell asleep after one loop.

On a pretty good day, it took two loops.

A difficult day required three loops.

An impossible day…well, you get the idea. Too much of this could drive a fellow loopy. I came to believe that the term *baby-sitting* should be replaced with *baby-walking*.

One day as I was walking Heather for the fourth time around the loop in the pouring rain—and me with a beastly, hacking chest cold—I was thinking that at times there isn't a whole lot of difference between being a father and being a slave on a Roman galley.

Little did I realize that my time at the oars was about to be doubled. From the moment our tiny girl started walking, Mom and Dad took to running. The whole pace of things around the house changed. A nervous electricity filled the air, as if a thousand invisible cattle prods stood ready to ambush any grownup who so much as thought of enjoying a moment's peace. It was like being in the old Wild West and never quite knowing when a cloud of painted ponies bearing whooping warriors might suddenly descend upon your homestead.

The very week Heather stood up wobblingly on her own two feet and took her first steps, pandemonium broke loose in our home. Enormous and bewildering forces swirled around our heads, and darkness seemed thick as soup. I had no idea what was going on at the time, but reflecting on this later, I found I had learned something. I learned that parents are often called upon to "cover" for their children—that is, to fight off the forces of evil while their little ones innocently make spectacular advances.

This season of struggle, like all trials, passed, and its passing was marked by the coming out of the sun. We'd had a rainy winter (not just outside but inside, reflected in the changing of countless diapers and the drying of countless tears), and not surprisingly our family had a touch of cabin fever. Now it was spring, and as our daughter learned to walk, nature turned cartwheels.

Never will I forget that first warm, sunny day when we took Heather outside and played with her on the grass. How wonderful to see our tiny girl against the magnificent backdrop of God's great outdoors and to watch as her little bare feet first touched real grass. It was almost like seeing her being born all over again.

Whatever the problems might be of coping with a new toddler, they seemed (for the moment) behind us. Today she was a real little girl. She stood on the solid earth, the green woods at her back and the great big blue sky forming a halo around her head. We could see in her eyes that she knew it herself: She knew she was a child of royalty, that somewhere she had a Daddy who owned the woods and the sky and everything else in the whole world and that He'd put it all there solely for her enjoyment.

Walking is a common metaphor for the spiritual life. We "walk in the way of righteousness" (Proverbs 8:20) along the "path of life" (Psalm 16:11). Perhaps it is no surprise that as children learn to walk, parents may feel that they too must return to fundamentals and learn again the art of putting one foot in front of another. For the parents of toddlers live no longer with both feet planted safely in the rational world. Instead they find themselves lured little by little, as by enchanted elves, into the prerational country of childhood, where life makes sense only as one sees it from a child's point of view. Like it or not, parents will experience the world much as their children do—all strange and wide and disorienting, the light too bright and the darkness overwhelming, never enough cuddles to absorb all the shocks, and everything good placed just out of reach.

I wonder: Is this what it was like for Jesus, accustomed to the perfection of heaven, to share the lot of human children in a dark and disorderly world? Are all parents called, in the very nature of the case, to inhabit chaos?

Living with young children means entering again into the nighttime terrors, the hard realities, and also the spontaneous, wild joys of a child's lot. Long and wistfully one may peer back at the sane and familiar adult world. But alas!—that world has become oddly unreachable. It's as if parents themselves are thrust back into the maelstrom of infancy, reduced to having brief attention spans frequently interrupted by shocks and traumas. When your toddler scrapes his knee and howls his head off, you too feel scraped and howling inside—especially if it happens while you're trying to cook supper and visit with in-laws.

A saintly woman once told me that having a child brings a couple face to face with reality. "Before becoming parents," she observed, "people live in a kind of dream world."

She's right. It takes children to make grownups of us.

We adults think young children require an enormous amount of energy and attention, but we feel this only because we ourselves have grown so fond of independence. Children charm us back into a proper balance of interdependence. While children pour their lives into ours without a thought, we grumble at having to return the favor. But children have it right: People thrive by lavishing attention upon one another.

One thing is certain: If we do not willingly give our children the right kind of attention, we shall be compelled to give the wrong kind. The time we do not spend caring and playing will be consumed in silencing complaints and doing damage control. Later on, when our kids are older, every hour we have not invested in loving them will be spent instead sitting in the offices of counselors, principals, and probation officers.

In other words, children expose our idols. Every time we think of a child as "interrupting" or "interfering with" our lives, it's because we have erected an idol in the place where love alone ought to reign. Ironically, our idol may be some task we think we are performing for the sake of our children, only to find that we have exchanged the God of living relationships for an isolating god of our own devising.

This is the gist of Jesus' rebuke to His disciples, "Let the little children come to me, and do not hinder them" (Luke 18:16). To let little children come to you, to be available with open and loving arms, is to let them come to Jesus. Often what keeps us from welcoming children is our own fanciful picture of what life is or should be like. Children continually challenge this picture. With little ones around we can no longer expect to "plan" our day as we used to. We can only plan to be available. Things aren't going to run on an even keel anymore because the even keel is an idol.

Children present us with this enigma: Are they flowers or are they weeds? Sitting still, they look like flowers, but as soon as they start spreading out, they can spoil the scenery. No matter how often we tidy up after them, they rally and spring back stronger than ever. Children have a stubborn taproot of disorder that is impossible to extricate. Would a flower throw tantrums and be rude to our guests?

Yes, children are a lot like weeds, yet in the long run we have to admit that these weeds are lovelier than the flowers. Children, like life itself, are the wildness that puts the most beautifully cultivated garden to shame.

Small children take naps every day. This is a good policy for all ages. Everyone has need not only for sleep but also for rest. Everyone has need not only for night dreams but for daydreams.

I know a mother of two who was having trouble relaxing on a weekend prayer retreat. While reading Scripture, she became agitated about the story in Mark 4 of Jesus' sleeping in the boat while His disciples were buffeted by a storm. Jesus' rebuke of His disciples for having so little faith especially troubled her.

The story continued to haunt her during a long walk, until finally in exasperation she prayed: "But Lord, what did You expect those men to do in the midst of that storm? They were in fear for their lives! Anyone would be. What did You expect them to do?"

To her surprise the Lord answered: "I expected them to lie down in the boat with Me and rest."

"Really?" she asked in amazement.

"Yes, really."

Would a loving heavenly Father put parents through the storm of toddlerhood without offering us the same rest and comfort He expects us to offer our children?

One evening while I was cleaning Heather's highchair and picking up all her things, it occurred to me that there must be angels assigned to us adults to perform similar duties, caring for us as we care for our children: tidying up our spiritual messes, picking up the various things we have carelessly discarded and strewn around—the shining garments, the helmets and breastplates, the swords left out in the rain to rust.

God knows that parents of toddlers don't have it easy. A friend of mine once had a dream in which she met Mary, the mother of Jesus. The dream seemed so real that long afterward my friend was able to give a startlingly vivid account.

"Mary was so sweet," she recalled. "A real sweetheart. She was only a little bit of a thing, quite short and slender, though not skinny. Petite, I'd call her. Maybe five foot three, just over a hundred pounds and every inch a lady."

According to this dream, Mary hadn't had an easy life. She told the dreamer she'd had many children besides Jesus (don't forget she started young) and that they weren't all as good as gold. One of them, to be sure, was God, but then there were all the other ones to drive her up the wall. Mary said that taking care of this unruly brood for all those years had taxed her to the absolute limit.

The dream ended with Mary's giving a personal message to my friend, who at that time was tearing out her hair while trying to keep pace with three preschoolers. Mary's message was this:

"You're a wonderful mother. You're doing a great job and your kids will turn out fine. Believe me, I know what it's like. My own kids drove me crazy, running wild and forever getting into things, squealing and squawking and scrapping all day long. I was the classic harried mom. Constantly I'd think, 'What does all this have to do with holiness?' Day after day I was driven to distraction. Yet somehow I found favor with God, and so have you. So take heart. Never call yourself a failure as a mother. It's not true. You're a beautiful mother, and don't let anyone tell you different."

# Chapter Two

# The Terrible Twos

*The infant will play near the hole of the cobra,*
*and the young child put his hand into the viper's nest.*

Isaiah 11:8

Children, let's face it, are not little angels. When Jesus pointed to a child and said, "Be like this," it's a good thing the kid wasn't having a temper tantrum.

Or is it? Was Jesus pointing to the child's good behavior or to something else? Good behavior, while a fruit of the gospel, has never been its heart.

At two I was a terrible child. I drove my mother to distraction. If I wanted her attention, I knew all I had to do was climb on top of the piano and shout at the top of my lungs, "JUMP, MOMMY, JUMP!"

At the sound of that bloodcurdling cry, from wherever she happened to be in the house—whether talking on the phone, trudging up the stairs with a load of laundry, or sitting on the toilet—my mother would instantly arise and come rushing to my rescue. And the moment she arrived on the scene, breathless and red-faced and shouting hysterically, "NO, MICHAEL, NO!" with a squeal of glee I would throw myself into her arms.

What is a mother to do with a monster like this? Not much. Such a child will take all your fine-sounding theories about parenting and eat them for breakfast. The only answer is to get up a little earlier in the morning and cry for help to the God who is more terrible than any two-year-old.

I like the word *terrible*. Isn't it a great word to describe God? The *King James Version* of Psalm 47:1-2 reads:

> O clap your hands, all ye people;
> > shout unto God with the voice of triumph.
> For the Lord most high is terrible;
> > he is a great King over all the earth.

To me the word *terrible* conjures up a God who hurls spitballs into space to create worlds, who is capable at any moment of upsetting our apple cart, of tearing the sky in two as if it were a piece of silk, or of casting the stars sizzling into the sea. This is a God to chant and shout to, to dance before, to worship in awe and trembling, and to follow with alacrity into any battle.

Why are we so bent on drumming out of children the very terribleness that reflects the character of God?

I'm seated at a kitchen table visiting a couple with a two-year-old. The kid is a living dynamo and the parents are tired. Very tired. They both hold down jobs, and with all the demands upon them they're barely keeping their noses above water.

Listen to a secret: I am the first adult they have invited into their home in six months. That's how stressed and bewildered they are. They cannot bear for anyone else to see how they live.

As the four of us sit there drinking tea, the parents watch every move of the terrible toddler, as if the spoon in her hand is a dangerous weapon and her mug a lethal missile. Their daughter's behavior is just what you'd expect from any ordinary, active child, yet to look at the parents, you'd think she was an escaped felon.

These are good, decent people. Without the kid they'd be your normal pleasant young sophisticates. With the kid, they are deeply ashamed and frightened. A two-year-old child is blowing their cover.

It's not just the bad behavior of children that gets under our skin. It's that whether they're bad or good they're like a bright light shining in our eyes, showing us up for who we are. As a child's consciousness grows, we're more and more aware of this other person in our home who sees the way we live—really sees—and who begins to judge the quality of our life as they catch on to some of our secrets, our vices, our skeletons in the closet. Not many of us are ready to have a little moral searchlight in our midst, illuminating the stains on our souls.

As a new father I was proud of my daughter, but I was more scared than proud. Scared because suddenly the awful shambles of my life were exposed. My little Heather was like a loud siren blaring away in my home, summoning the thought police, the ancestors, the apocalyptic angels. Such unrelenting scrutiny was enough to drive a person mad.

Babies are bad enough. When babies start appearing in a home, many people seek refuge in depression. But a two-year-old is a scandal, an offense, an affront to common decency. Children make us ashamed of ourselves because we wish our lives were better for their sake. We wish we could be their heroes instead of their oppressors.

Once in a McDonald's restaurant I watched a man at the counter with his two toddlers. No mother was in sight. The dad was in the process of collecting his order when suddenly the two kids took their tall drinks and set off in search of a table.

Dad wasn't ready for this. Probably he'd assumed they would all move to their table in an orderly family unit. How wrong he was! There he stood at the counter with his wallet open, while his two charges took off for who knows where with big, wet drinks balanced shakily in their tiny paws. Dad, like a little child himself, was left all alone, abandoned. Too much was happening all at once...

As it turned out, nothing did happen. No drinks were spilled; the children did not fall off the end of the earth. But I wish I'd had a camera to record the expression on this man's face—a look of primal, wide-eyed terror—as a perfectly normal, but unanticipated, scene unfolded before his eyes. You'd have thought he was watching Godzilla tear apart his car.

Why are adults so frightened of mere children? It's because

children know no law except the desires of their own hearts. That's why they will blunder headlong toward an open stairwell without any thought of personal danger. What can happen? At worst, a little bump or two, and then loving arms will scoop them up to safety.

A child trusts. What fanaticism!

Of course such a freewheeling lifestyle has its problems, but it also has awesome advantages. A child knows instinctively that there is grace for making any number of mistakes, hence forgiveness flows as easily as breath. In this system, every day really is brand-new. Every moment is brand-new. If a little grape juice spills on a white carpet—hey, no big deal. By the time the juice is out of the cup, it's already a thing of the past, over and forgotten.

Children represent a new world order. Their lives declare plainly and stridently that there is a radically different way to go about life, a way that lies right under our noses but that we adults disdainfully ignore. After all, we big people have the power. No race of bothersome little aliens is going to show us how to live.

But show us they do, and it's unsettling. More than anyone else in the world, except the true prophets and evangelists of God, children threaten the comfortable world system that enmeshes the rest of us so idiotically. Children live as if there are no rules, as if they have been reading the New Testament and discovered that the law with all its complex code of regulations and restrictions has been canceled, taken away, nailed to the dead wood of the cross.

Life rushes at a child full bore like a waterfall. Rules are like a faucet on the waterfall. Who needs them?

Heather was a terrible child, make no mistake about it. She wasn't just a terrible two, but a terrible three, four, five, and so on. She seemed so different from Karen and me, as if cut from another cloth. Since our lives were so blessed in other ways, perhaps we needed this one area of struggle to keep us humble. When the going got really tough, it occurred to me that God must be punishing us with Heather.

What heresy! Yet like all heresies, this one held a grain of truth. A child's terribleness is meant to expand our vision, challenge the limits of our small world, invite and push us into the very areas of our weakness and woundedness. Do kids upset us and cramp our style? Good! The ways that people do not fit our mold are precisely the ways they can bless us. Our Heather had been perfectly chosen and designed to bless us by leading us further into the staggering immensity of reality.

No one in their right mind would have invented children. They are too impractical, too unwieldy, too preposterous. Intelligent people sat down and came up with wonderful inventions like the light bulb, the telephone, the printing press, but no one would have dreamed of designing and patenting a child. Even if they had, it would have been a diaperless child, a noncrying child, a well-behaved and obedient child. Inventions are meant (at least in theory) to make life easier, not harder. They are conveniences.

Children are not convenient. This is the difference between an invention and a creation. Inventions simplify, codify, organize what is known, whereas creations present us with the unknown. Creations are larger than life, inventions are smaller. Creations transgress all scientific laws and reasonable limits, bursting the bounds of reality itself and so glorifying God. But inventions, by and large, obscure God. With an invention in our hands, we have no need of God. We are in control.

With a terrible child running around the house, suddenly our inventions seem inconsequential. Suddenly we need God again.

Parents of small children may regard their work as mundane and exasperating, but their job will never be replaced by a machine—which is more than one can say for many other jobs. We may dream of the time when a handy little robot will be invented to do all our housework, but this will never happen because household tasks are too difficult for machines. We have automated car factories, but we'll never see a robot capable of stuffing a pillowcase, to say nothing of diapering a baby. Not only is parenting too difficult for a machine, it's too difficult for many a corporate executive (not to mention a writer of Christian books).

There's no work more complex, more important, or more exalted than that of caring for children. After all, it's what God Himself has chosen, above all else, to do with His time.

Yes, as adorable and fascinating as children are, caring for them can be so taxing that one hardly has time to enjoy them. But doesn't the same paradox lie at the core of life itself? We know full well that we live charmed lives in a wondrous universe, yet our actual experience of daily existence can seem dreary and burdensome. Why can't we enjoy ourselves more? Why can't we enjoy our kids more? Do we have to wait to become grandparents before we begin to relish the terrible glory of it all?

For a child who used to terrorize his mother, I grew up, mysteriously, to be a rather passive adult. Somewhere along the line the terribleness got knocked out of me. What happened?

I suspect I left some of it on the playground in grade seven when I thought I could beat up the class bully. I forget how the fight started, only that it ended with my lying on my back in the snow for over an hour while he sat on top of me until I cried "uncle."

It was cold and wet in the snow. I had a lot of time to think about my powerlessness and to soak up the opposite of terribleness, shame. As determined as I was not to give in, finally I did. I wanted to go home, get warm and dry, have supper.

So much for terribleness. No mommy to catch me when I jumped that time.

I've watched this same process, the insidious encroachment of shame, in Heather's life. At the age of nine, for example, she foolishly picked a fight with an older, bigger boy. In a few seconds she got herself thoroughly thrashed and ran home, her glasses bent, crying tears of shock and outrage.

"I really thought I could beat him," she told me later. A passionate fan of *Star Wars*, with wide, unblinking eyes she said wistfully, "I thought the Force was with me."

I no longer want to climb on top of pianos and threaten to jump, but here's what I do desire: I want to revert to my terrible twos. I want to recover some of that healthy, boundless, natural energy that can set a toddler to shouting, singing, tumbling, charging through life as if—heaven help us!—life were meant to be celebrated and enjoyed to the full.

I'd like to capture the spirit of that tiny dynamo in a bottle and take a few swigs of it every day. I'd like a swig of terribleness before I sit down to write, another one upon entering that modern graveyard called the mall, another one before talking to Heather about her first date. I want the terrible largeness of reality to live in my bones and the grandeur of creation to set fire to my blood every waking moment. I want to roar into my world like an express train barreling home.

I want to live not in fear of myself or others, but in the fear—yes, that old-fashioned word—of my awesome and terrible God.

And for you, Heather, I desire a double dose of terribleness. I bless you to be a holy terror.

# THE THREE FOOLS: A STORY

*The star they had seen in the east went ahead of them*
*until it stopped over the place where the child was.*

MATTHEW 2:9

The three wise men (as everyone knows but likes to forget) did not visit Jesus in the manger as a baby. They found Him much later, living in a shanty on the outskirts of Bethlehem, when He was two years old. This is important.

They were looking for a child, and this was a matter of some awkwardness for them. They wondered: *What sort of behavior would be appropriate in the presence of a child-king?*

They pictured themselves kneeling, presenting their gifts, and then perhaps sitting stiffly on the edge of wooden chairs and sipping tea. Their conversation would be mainly with the parents, of course, while the child looked on serenely, wonderingly. With careful humility they would avoid His large, omniscient eyes.

This is not how things turned out.

These men were bachelors, remember. Monkish types.

Contemplatives used to sitting on their duffs and reaching after the ineffable with their noggins. What could they possibly have known about the terrible twos?

How surprised the Magi were to find their little king blazing around the house in a torn toga, chattering up a storm and leaping onto their laps to tweak their beards. Even more surprising, they found they did not react to these improprieties with horror. Instead they felt all the stiffness draining out of them, lifetimes of reverent caution (i.e., distrust) melting like marshmallows in hot chocolate. They were charmed, delighted, won. Truly and deeply.

In no time they found themselves regressing, relaxing back into the childhoods they had never had. They got down on their knees, all right, but not to worship—it was to give the child camel rides on their backs and then to roll over like great, fat bears while the boy who had made the universe used their bellies for trampolines. Yes, they fell down before their king, yet not in some formal act of prostration, but felled like bowling pins by the thunder of a child's chortle.

People who have had no childhoods are old at forty. They have lived their lives, they can see no way forward. They can only go back to where they have never been, and this prospect is terribly frightening.

Imagine being frightened of becoming a child. It's like being frightened of ice cream. But just so did things stand with the Magi. Even the stars—which to the Boy King were like so many marbles, so many toy jewels for scattering and gathering—were to these men objects of utmost seriousness. Had they not given themselves to following a star, believing this to be the great high purpose of their lives? And where had it gotten them?

Rolling around in their sumptuous robes on the dirt floor of a hovel, that's where. Squealing like pigs, hooting till their sides fairly split, squirting out buckets of snotty tears. Ripping open their fine silks and brocades so that the holy little hoodlum could blow trumpet kisses into their bare tums. Years later they would still feel the amazing soft violence of His kiss in their navels, as if He really had found an aperture there and played them like an instrument, blown them full of brassy jubilance.

"Say, little fellow, you're pretty full of beans, aren't you?"

"You better believe I am!" said His laughing eyes. "Now you open wide your mouths, your ears, your hands, and your hearts, because I'm going to fill you up with beans too."

And He did. They gave Him their tawdry treasures; He gave them beans. A bean for rib-tickling; a bean for wrestling; a bean for giggling and guffawing; a bean for indignity; a bean for innocence and one for dance.

Did the Magi know beyond doubt that they had found their king? Oh yes, they knew! They knew it when the little guy sat astride their backs, smacked them on the rumps, and cried, "Giddyap, Frankincense! Mush, Myrrh! Hi ho, Gold—away!"

"Jesus, hon," His mother kept saying, "don't embarrass the nice men."

But He was born to embarrass nice men, to embarrass them with riches. All day long the great sages lay in the dirt, collapsed in ecstasy, slain by the spirit of an urchin. All night they lay there too, babbling in tongues, humming snatches of psalms and Mother Goose, burbling musically like babes. That night the greatest astrologers of the ancient world literally saw stars—saw them for the first time, as they are, rolling round heaven to a toddler's tune.

These men who had come to pray, ended in play. They came to give gifts but ended by leaving what they had long ached to be rid of: starched collars, tinsel crowns, jaded adult wisdom. That first Epiphany, wise men turned into wise guys, jokers. They became fools—fools for Christ.

# CHAPTER THREE

# HOW CHILDREN LEAD

*The wolf will live with the lamb,*
*the leopard will lie down with the goat,*
*the calf and the lion and the yearling together;*
*and a little child will lead them.*

ISAIAH 11:6

My three-year-old neighbor, Grace, has Down's syndrome. She is also a survivor of leukemia. That's a lot to pack into three years.

While I was writing this book another neighbor of mine, Bob, was going through a difficult time. He'd developed a heart problem that drastically curtailed his lifestyle. He tried everything to get better: doctors, diet, books, prayer, meditation. He sought to eliminate every scrap of negative stress from his life. Still the pain persisted.

Frustrated and bewildered, Bob begged God both for healing and for wisdom, for some insight into how to cope. Weeks, months went by with no word, no change. Silence.

One sunny afternoon in September I was chatting with Bob outside his house. Out of the corner of my eye I saw little Grace across the way. All of a sudden she began running toward us, her pudgy legs pumping and her arms outstretched wide. Was she chasing a ball, or what? It looked like she was planning to barrel right through us. Sure enough, with her round shining face uplifted in ecstasy, she plowed straight into Bob and threw her arms around him.

A hug. She just wanted to give Bob a big hug.

Wow! I had no idea Bob had developed such a great relationship with this little girl. I was impressed.

At this point Bob suddenly lost all interest in our conversation and, looking dazed, went over to the grass and lay down on his back. It was one of those gorgeous autumn days when the sun still has the warmth of summer. Apparently Bob just wanted to relax and soak up some rays, but Grace was still there and she wasn't about to leave him alone. She lay down on top of him and began kissing his cheeks. Then she bounced up and down on his belly.

Seeing this, Grace's dad came over with a worried look on his face.

"Gracie, what are you doing?" he said. "Leave Bob alone. He doesn't want you bouncing all over him."

"No, no, it's okay," muttered Bob.

As I left, Grace was still bouncing while Bob gazed up into the sun-drenched sky, looking at once both dumbfounded and blissful, as if he'd just been kissed by an angel.

About a week later Bob told me what had really happened that day. It turned out that prior to this he'd had no special relationship with Grace. To him she was just another kid in the neighborhood.

She'd never hugged him before, never paid him any particular attention.

But Bob had been seeking God for a word, a message. Desperately. For weeks.

Suddenly a child named Grace runs up to him out of the blue and hugs him. Covers him with kisses, jumps all over him, and won't leave him alone, as if she's madly in love with him or something.

"In that moment," Bob said, "God spoke to me. He said *I love you.* He spoke it right into my heart. Simple, but profound. The message came home so deeply it shook me. I couldn't stand up anymore. I had to go over and lie on the grass. But then I began to have doubts. Is this really God? Is He really speaking to me? And then it came again, and kept coming and coming. I couldn't get over it. More hugs, more kisses. *I love you, I love you, I love you...*"

Grace.

Love.

A message from God.

From a little child.

With Down's syndrome.

A survivor of leukemia.

Three years old.

Did Bob get the message?

You bet.

But it's still hard.

Many months after this incident Bob still has heart problems.

But a little child is leading him.

Children lead, as adults should, primarily by action and example. How beautifully simple it all appears when the behavior of a child fleshes out before our eyes the great secrets of faith. When we grasp that we too are but children, decades of strain and worry fall away from us like winter clothes tossed aside in spring.

Of course, children don't always act as shining exemplars of grace and love. In our journey to childlike faith, it is too simplistic to suggest that all we have to do is model the behavior of a child. Children are too bad for that.

Nevertheless, God can speak to us through children even in their badness. We may learn a great deal from the wholesomeness of children, their spontaneous goodness and love, their quickness to forgive. Yet oddly enough, whether children are good or bad, cute or nasty, they can teach us just as much because small children are not bad in the way we are. Their frank, open badness illumines our own more subtle and secretive corruption. Children don't bog down in sin as we do. They can be horrible one moment and sweet as pie the next. In their naive transparency they present us with a mirror image of the spiritual life.

For example, at three Heather was quick to say "Sorry," but the word didn't yet mean for her what it meant for me. I wanted her to accept responsibility for the fact that by being bad she had broken intimacy with me, but for Heather this concept did not compute. Her "sorry" had less to do with restoring relationship than with escaping punishment.

This led me to ponder my own motives in repentance. When I say "sorry" to God, am I just trying to get off the hook and avoid consequences? Or is the quality of my relationship with my Divine Lover so precious that I am sensitive to every small break in intimacy with Him?

Hear now another parable of the kingdom:

For several years Heather had a habit that drove Karen and me crazy. Whenever we tried to tell her something she didn't want to hear, Heather would block her ears. She would literally put her hands over her ears and refuse to listen.

Sometimes we'd be bawling her out for bad behavior. Other times we'd just want to talk over some problem she was facing and offer wise counsel. Yet no matter how gently and lovingly we spoke, if Heather didn't want to listen, up went her hands like the drawbridge to a castle. She sealed the fortress and there was no getting through.

We tried everything. We sent her to her room. We shouted louder. We punished her for blocking her ears. We forbade her to do it. We physically, forcibly removed her hands from her ears. And so on.

Nothing worked.

This behavior persisted until one time when Heather was struggling with making friends. Gently I tried pointing out to her how some of her actions might be hurting or alienating potential friends. I'd said no more than two or three sentences, when not only did she plug her ears but she burst into enraged tears, fled upstairs, and barricaded herself in her room.

At an earlier stage this behavior might have prompted me to run after her and force open the door, yelling, "Heather, whether you want to or not, you're going to listen to this!" (Like father, like daughter.) But we were past that now. On this occasion, though I still followed her upstairs, instead of pounding on her door, I prayed. Without saying a word I simply sat in the hallway outside her door and prayed.

After a while I said quietly, "Heather, I love you," or something like that. No response. A minute later I tried again, and then again. It wasn't hard to be patient and to speak to her gently and kindly because I was feeling the gentle, loving presence of the Holy Spirit.

Still Heather would not respond. For about ten minutes she continued to give me the silent treatment.

Then, slowly, the door opened a crack, and the next moment she was rushing into my arms.

After that I could freely tell her all that I wanted her to hear.

Later, alone in my room, I was wrestling in prayer with a different problem. But I couldn't get anywhere, something blocked my prayers. When I asked, "What is it, Lord?" immediately I recalled Jesus saying, "Here I am! I stand at the door and knock. If anyone hears my voice and opens the door, I will come in" (Revelation 3:20).

All at once I realized that at that very moment Jesus was sitting outside my door, praying and speaking lovingly to me. I'd assumed I wanted fellowship with Jesus when really I was barricaded in my room! As I opened the door and rushed into His arms, He communicated the same message I'd been trying to tell Heather, pointing out to me the ways I was alienating people and sabotaging potential friendships.

The moral: Listen closely to the advice you give your children, for it may be the word of the Lord to you. It takes one to know one. If you are bothered by certain problems in your children, it's likely you have these same problems yourself and have passed them on. Address these issues in your own life and then you will know how to help your children. If you want to reach your kids, lower your own drawbridge.

You long for your children to listen to you, but do you listen to them? Or do you plug your ears? Do you let children lead you? Do you let them lead you in supposedly adult matters, such as prayer?

Perhaps you find yourself tearing out your hair because for years you've tried to establish a tradition of family prayers, but your kids won't cooperate. Worse still, maybe they do cooperate and every day like clockwork your family reads the Bible and prays, but there's no life in it.

What to do? Ponder Luke 11:1: "One day Jesus was praying in a certain place. When he finished, one of his disciples said to him, 'Lord, teach us to pray, just as John taught his disciples.'"

I find this request startling: It clearly implies that up to this point Jesus had not been teaching His disciples how to pray. Apparently there were no nightly devotions, no Scripture meditation, no group prayer times in which Jesus encouraged the disciples to pray aloud. Nothing like that. Instead Jesus withdrew to pray alone, leaving His disciples also to pray alone.

This was the normal pattern. Until eventually, with miracles popping all over the place, one disciple became curious enough, bold and humble enough to approach Jesus and ask, "Lord, teach us to pray."

Had Jesus been waiting a long time for this moment? Clearly He never forced it. He never gathered His disciples around the table and said, "Okay, kids, whether you like it or not, we're now going to have family prayers." In many areas of life Jesus gave disturbingly plain instructions. But on the subject of group prayer He apparently held His tongue. In fact He said, "When you pray, go into your room, close the door and pray to your Father, who is unseen" (Matthew 6:6).

Evidently Jesus felt there was something essentially secret about prayer. Only when deliberately probed did He begin to divulge its secrets.

We adults need to ask ourselves: Are miracles occurring all around us in a way that draws the curiosity even of children, those original skeptics? Is the quality of our life such that our children come to us to find out what our secret is?

Jesus said, "Let the little children come to me" (Luke 18:16). Interestingly He did not say, "Go to them" (though obviously we're to do this too). Jesus was more concerned with capitalizing on the teachable moment by letting children take the lead in coming to Him.

The problem with adults is that we know too much. We're too

set in our ways. If only we could forget everything we know and truly kneel, truly get down to the level of a child, maybe then we'd know how to lead our children by letting them lead us. Maybe then we'd say to them, "Teach us to pray."

I've never forgotten the time Heather said to me, "Dad, your prayers are too long." From that point on I deliberately sought to shorten them. This was hard for me, like having a tough editor who wanted to make drastic cuts to my beloved book manuscript. But now each night as I knelt beside Heather's bed, I gradually became more aware of the presence of the Holy Spirit. In time this felt presence became so strong, so overwhelming, that often I could not think of anything to pray. At such times words were not needed. Just being with Heather and with God was enough. In this way I got a foretaste of the beautiful prayer of quiet into which the Lord, through a child, was leading me.

# BIG AND LITTLE

*When I was a child, I talked like a child,*
*I thought like a child, I reasoned like a child.*
*When I became a man, I put childish ways behind me.*

1 CORINTHIANS 13:11

One day I caught Heather standing on a chair and reaching up into the medicine cabinet to get a bottle of pills.

Is this a picture of you? Are you always trying to make yourself bigger than you are, reaching too high for strong spiritual medicine that could be dangerous for you? Are you God's child or His adult?

In the verse quoted above it sounds as if Paul is saying, "It's time to grow up and become a man." But actually he means just the opposite. The next verse makes it clear that in this world our potential is limited because we "know in part" and "see but a poor reflection as in a mirror." Since we will not reach full maturity until heaven, in spiritual terms we are meant for now to live as children, to think like children, to embrace childish ways.

Even mature believers are still only children. John in his first epistle addresses his readers ten times as "dear children," a phrase Jesus and Paul also use. Yet in our times childhood is disappearing, not only in society but in the church. Following the lead of our fast-paced, overworked culture, we take on too much responsibility too soon. We walk before we can crawl, and run when we ought to be nursing at the breast. Believers seem to like the idea of being "born again," but who is prepared to be a child again?

As a parent I'm impressed by how long it takes for a child to grow to maturity. Each stage has its appropriate capabilities, and the process cannot, must not, be rushed. God took eighty years to prepare Moses to lead the people of Israel, and Jesus Himself did not begin His ministry until the age of thirty. Yet today we worry about Christians in their twenties who do not yet know what to do with their lives.

Have you had your thirty hidden years yet? Or are you one of those Christians who grew up too fast and never had a childhood?

"Like newborn babies," wrote Peter, "crave pure spiritual milk, so that by it you may grow up in your salvation, now that you have tasted that the Lord is good" (1 Peter 2:2-3). Many Christians work hard for God but no longer taste His goodness. Unwilling to live with the uncertainty of waiting on the Lord, they pretend to know His will prematurely. When the true call does come, they're too busy to hear it.

Throughout my Christian life my greatest failing has been pretending to know too much. In church I pretend to know what to do. In prayer meetings I pretend to know what to pray. In social gatherings I pretend to know how to conduct myself. Even with good friends I may put on an appearance of being relaxed and intimate when really I do not feel that way.

Doesn't growing up mean having to pretend more and more that we know what is going on? We're big boys and girls now, aren't we? And other people seem to know the ropes, don't they? Why do I feel so clueless? Obviously I'd better get with it!

Knowing too much is the bane of our sophisticated, technological society. Under all the pressure to conform, to grow up, to get on with the show, we end up settling for a life of pretense rather than holding out for authenticity.

Tragically, by living such a lie we can never afford to let down our guard enough to depend on God. Our pretentiousness shows up in our failure to ask for everything we need. Instead we pretend either that we have no needs or that our needs are beyond His sphere of competence. Rather than trusting God to look after us, we assume that we can and should be looking after ourselves. When we find that we cannot, we're always surprised, embarrassed, shocked.

O Lord, help me! Help me to see that I am "wretched, pitiful, poor, blind and naked" (Revelation 3:17). Help me to know my littleness in order to discover Your bigness!

My little daughter taught me littleness, but not in the way one might expect. Heather herself had trouble with littleness. No doubt this was rooted in my own controlling nature, for children emulate their parents. In any case, far from being a trusting, compliant child, Heather has always acted too big for her britches.

At the age of three and a half she knew everything. Sometimes I would deliberately ask her whether she knew something that I knew she didn't know. She always said yes.

"Heather, does this house have an attic?"

"Yes."

"Do you know what an attic is?"

"Yes."

"What is it?"

"Ummmm…"

Similarly, at the approach of Heather's bedtime I'd say to her three or four times, "Heather, you should be in bed by now."

In an irritated tone she would answer, "Dad, I *know*"—and then return contentedly to whatever she was doing.

Whenever this happened I'd think, or sometimes I'd say out loud, "No, Heather, you don't know. If you knew, you'd be in bed. The fact that you are still up shows that you do not know what I am talking about." I wish I had a nickel for every time Heather has said "I know" about something she does know but isn't doing anything about.

Ironically, through this behavior I came to see that I was acting the same way with God. How often did the Lord speak to me and I answered, "Yes, Lord, I know," and then go on merrily about my business?

Isn't this a problem for most Christians? My hunch is that about 5 percent of what we think we know about God (our theology) is genuinely helpful in our pursuit of holiness. As for the rest,

I've a sneaking suspicion it's a clever human plot for sidestepping the divine will.

Finally the day came when I got Heather to say the sweet words, "I don't know." Her best friend was a girl named Sheri who was two years her senior. Sheri was a hyperactive girl with a lot of exaggerated mannerisms. For a while Heather was emerging from playtimes talking and acting exactly like Sheri, from head to toe a perfect imitation. At first, I think, this behavior was unconscious, but then she began doing it deliberately and we all found it screamingly funny.

One day I said, "Heather, can you do an imitation of Heather now? What does Heather sound like? How does Heather look?"

For long moments she stared blankly into space. Finally, soundly perplexed, she said the words that were music to my ears: "I don't know."

During the writing of this book I realized that God had been waiting a long time to hear from me these same three sweet little words, "I don't know." Come to think of it, I'd been waiting a long time myself to muster enough courage to make this confession. Some people have a tape inside them that says, "I'm stupid and I don't know anything." My problem has always been the opposite. My tape says, "I know."

I was surprised at how wonderfully delicious it felt to reverse this tape and learn to say the opposite words—"I don't know." For several months this simple phrase became the theme of all my prayers. I'd sit and mumble it over and over like a babbling idiot, or should I say like a babbling brook? Gradually its gentle music drained away from me all pressure to know anything I did not truly know, to be anything I could not be, to do anything not given me to do.

No prayer is more powerful than the prayer of powerlessness, of littleness, of not knowing. Isn't this what it means to be poor in spirit? "Knowledge puffs up," wrote Paul, "but love builds up. The man who thinks he knows something does not yet know as he ought to know. But the man who loves God is known by God" (1 Corinthians 8:1-3).

Before learning the "I don't know" prayer, I wasn't even aware of the degree of self-effort in my life. But the signs of it were there in the form of anxiety, frustration, insecurity, and a thought life that often whirled out of control. Though I spent a good deal of time praying, issues I could not resolve dominated my prayers. I would worry problems to death rather than admit my helplessness and humbly ask for help.

Many people combat this problem in prayer by employing a phrase or a single word (such as *Jesus* or *love*) to center their thoughts. There are biblical grounds for this practice. For example, we're told that the four living creatures in the throne room of heaven cry out day and night, "Holy, holy, holy is the Lord God Almighty" (Revelation 4:8).

My simple three-word prayer did more to lift me into the throne room of God than all my years of pious verbiage. What better way for the Holy Spirit to prepare me to write *The Mystery of Children* than by gently circumventing my rigid adult thinking, scrubbing clean my mental hard drive, and restoring me to a state of helpless wonder?

For me the beginning of childlike faith was when God became so big that I could no longer think complex theological thoughts about Him, but could only mumble and muse, stammer and sigh. I was learning the alphabet of praise.

To be a child is to know, beyond any doubt or question, that some things are bigger than you are.

The universe, for example, is bigger than you. Philosophers sit in judgment upon the universe, presuming to comprehend reality with their minds. But when you're a child, your relationship with reality is not rational but charmed. The universe is quite obviously bigger than you.

Similarly, you know that adults are bigger than you. Adults are taller, heavier, older, more skilled and experienced. They are even wiser in their own way. You know this. You know it even when adults are not trustworthy, even when you disobey and try to get your own way. Deep down you know that you are up against something bigger than you.

This is why children go to school automatically. If you go to church, you go because it's there. You do not question these rituals any more than you question whether the sun will come up in the morning.

Of course, at a certain age this all changes. The change begins with doubts, subtle questions, first at the feeling level and later at the intellectual level. This skepticism is natural because to grow up is to become bigger in every way. When you start feeling bigger than the things around you, from your new perspective you cannot help but look back and evaluate and make judgments.

This gets confusing. Is it really okay to judge things that used to be bigger than you? Are you truly big enough to take on your parents, the school system, or your society?

In Alice's first adventure in Wonderland she takes a drink that makes her suddenly grow tall. Then she eats a cake and becomes smaller than a mouse. Drinking and eating by turns, she gets big, then little, then big again. But she cannot seem to become the size she wants—exactly the right size to pass through a certain doorway into a beautiful garden.

This is what it's like to grow up. You change so quickly that you're no longer sure of your relative size in comparison to everything around you. From now on you're always either too big or too little to get where you want to be. How can you move around in a world where you no longer know what's big and what's little? Things were a lot easier when you looked up at the stars and knew you didn't have to understand them, because God did and somehow that was the same as you understanding.

Doubts about relative size are paralyzing, and many people remain paralyzed all their lives. They can never quite decide, for instance, whether or how it might be appropriate to evaluate their parents. Yet as long as they withhold judgment, they also withhold forgiveness. Hence they are stuck forever with parents who are too big to relate to.

The same happens in our relationship with God. At a certain stage we must establish which of us is bigger. Yet how can we believe in God while at the same time asking the questions about Him that beg to be asked? Many people handle this dilemma by deciding once and for all that they needn't believe in God because they have grown bigger than He, when really they have only outgrown old concepts of Him.

Jesus said, "Be as shrewd as snakes and as innocent as doves" (Matthew 10:16). As adults we may have decided to be as shrewd as snakes about everything, leaving no room at all for innocence. At what point in our lives did this happen? When did we stop trusting, and how can we recover trust? How can we begin to relax our cynicism and allow ourselves to be little and vulnerable?

Trust will not return of its own accord. One must choose to trust. This choice is the essence of faith. Faith is a decision to accept our littleness in relation to God. As John the Baptist said of Jesus, "He must become greater; I must become less" (John 3:30).

If some problem seems bigger than I am, so big as to be overwhelming, the truth is that I am making myself bigger than the problem. I am trying to solve it in my own strength. Making myself small, I see how to handle it.

Littleness has a feel to it. I know the real thing because it feels safe, comfortable, right. Knowing I'm little, I find myself smiling sweetly and laughing easily, and at night I sleep like a baby.

The prophet Amos had two visions in which he saw terrible judgments from God falling upon Israel, one a plague of locusts, the other in the form of fire. In each case Amos pleaded with the Lord to change His mind, interceding for his nation not because of its goodness but solely on the basis of its smallness: "Sovereign LORD, I beg you, stop! How can Jacob survive? He is so small!" Hearing this prayer, "the LORD relented" (Amos 7:5-6).

In situations where I feel angry, worried, afraid, or alienated, I'm learning to ask myself: How am I playing at being big here? How might it be possible to relax and let myself be small?

Prayer is the process of crouching down and making ourselves small before God. This downsizing is not an option; it is the only way to enter the kingdom of heaven. To grow in the Spirit is to become little in relation to more and more areas of life—marriage, family, church, work—until eventually it is possible to be little and childlike even in the presence of Satan and all his demons. For it is God, not you or I, who is bigger than evil.

At times in my Christian life I've felt like a bear cornered by dogs and hunters. The going gets rough, darkness closes in, demons hiss in my ear, even fellow Christians seem to attack me behind my back. In such a situation my instinct is to rise up, bristling, to my full height and face my attackers with bared teeth and slashing claws. But of course, puffing myself up only makes me a bigger target, an easier prey.

Sensing this, all at once I see a different solution. Peering down from my towering height, I spy a tiny doorway at my feet, a door so small as to be barely noticeable. A door, as it were, hidden beneath a fallen leaf on the forest floor. Crouching down to investigate, I see that if I make myself very small I might just manage to squeeze through this doorway. Even as this thought crosses my mind, the tiny door seems to open and I catch a glimpse of where it leads. It leads into a ravishingly beautiful, flower-studded meadow far away from all of my troubles and enemies.

Will I take this escape route? Will I accept the humility of retreat?

All these thoughts flash through my mind in a split second. Meanwhile my enemies are poised to pounce, including the worst enemy of all—my own angry aggression—which is about to unleash its full fury within me. I don't have a moment to lose. If I'm not to be overcome, I must instantly make a choice.

So I do. Instead of puffing myself up, I decide to collapse myself and squeeze through the small doorway. Although I'm a man and this feels like a door for a mouse, or even a louse, nevertheless I picture that beautiful meadow of freedom on the other side, and I go for it.

The moment I do—the moment I actually humble myself—I begin to feel the wind in my hair. For I'm running now, running through that flowery meadow with God's great open sky above me and sunshine all around, and before I know it, I'm rolling and laughing in the long grass with the flowers brushing my cheeks.

And then I'm at peace. Warm, still, relaxed, amazed. Safe in the arms of littleness.

# THE SEARCH FOR LOVE

*Dear children, let us not love with words or tongue*
*but with actions and in truth.*

1 JOHN 3:18

To develop childlike faith one must love a child, for we take on the likeness of what we love. If we loved children more, we wouldn't mind being one ourselves.

In *The Little Prince,* Antoine de Saint-Exupéry writes:

I know a planet where there is a certain red-faced gentleman. He has never smelled a flower. He has never looked at a star. He has never loved anyone. He has never done anything in his life but add up figures. And all day he says over and over, just like you, "I am busy with matters of consequence!" And that makes him swell up with pride. But he is not a man—he is a mushroom![2]

When my daughter was four years old, this statement largely described me, except for one detail: I did not add up figures. No, my father had spent his life adding up figures, and I would have none of that. To this day, show me a figure and I'll run away. After all, I'm an artist, quite above all that. Engaged in matters of consequence!

Instead of adding up figures, I add up words. My dictionary defines *mason* as "a skilled worker who builds by laying units of substantial material." True to my name, I take little words and lay them one after another into sentences, paragraphs, books. Row upon row, page after page of words, words, words.

When Heather was four, this was not only my trade and calling but my chief passion, the thing that made me swell with pride.

Meanwhile my little girl (my little princess!) was calling out for my love.

Heather and I are sitting on the couch reading a story. I'm edgy. I've spent longer with her than I'd intended. Right after this she's supposed to have a nap. Will she comply? Will I get some time to myself this afternoon? Goodness knows, she ought to be tired—she kept us up late enough last night! She should be nodding off soon; why isn't she looking more sleepy…?

The story ends. I close the book. Wide-awake, Heather suddenly looks straight at me and says, "You don't love me. Mommy loves me. But you don't."

What? These words cut me to the quick. What on earth is she talking about?

The truth is, I know exactly what she's talking about. Her words provoke two reactions in me, one near the surface, the other deeper down, so deep it's hidden almost from me. The shallow thought is: What does she mean? The deeper, instinctive reaction is: How did she know?

After all, I've been so good, haven't I? I've tried so hard. I've worked so diligently to cover up my lovelessness. Are all these efforts worth nothing? I mean, didn't I just make lunch for her, play with her, read her a story? Is it possible she can see through all this? Are children really that intelligent? Is this child smarter than I am? Can I not outwit her? Is there nowhere to hide? I feel the way I suppose Heather might feel if I happened into the kitchen just at the point when she is reaching for a forbidden cookie: I know I've been caught. Red-handed.

But all this comes to me later. For now, choosing to avoid the depths and stick to the shallows, I ask Heather innocently, lamely, "What do you mean, honey?"

This is my favorite method of evading truth: Act dumb. Put on a cloak of confusion.

But Heather isn't fooled. She's not playing that game. Instead of answering my question she climbs up onto the back of the couch, stares out the window, and exclaims, "Look at the clouds!" Already her face has changed from the open, frank flower of a moment before to a flesh-colored stone wall. It's the face of a sphinx, a sibyl: the depthless, inscrutable mask of childhood.

After this there's no getting her back to the subject of whether or not I love her. For one brief moment a window had opened onto a mystery. Then it closed again as softly as an eyelid, leaving no trace of any eye beneath.

A few minutes later, as I'm tucking her in for her nap, I say, "You know, Heather, I don't love you the way Mommy loves you. I love you in a different way. My own way."

And I leave it at that. But I know this answer doesn't satisfy. In my mind I keep rationalizing, working out convincing explanations. For example: "Heather, it may be true that at that moment of this particular day I wasn't loving you very well. You're right that my mind was elsewhere. But in general, that is, overall, if you see what I mean, the fact is..." and so on.

Nothing washes.

Heather's words continued to trouble me all that day and on through the night. Until the next afternoon, during her nap—a time that was normally precious to me for doing my work—I found myself spending a long time sitting in her room while she slept. I prayed, but my prayer was like a dream in which you repeat the same senseless action over and over, without getting anywhere.

God did not speak to me. There was no measurable result.

Except that later, for some reason, I told Heather what I'd done: that because of what she said, I'd spent her nap time praying in her room about love. This impressed her. Not that I'd been trying to impress her; I told her I hadn't come up with any answers. Still, something relaxed between us, and after that things got better. Much better.

Maybe true love begins with simply admitting—to God, to yourself, and to your child—that you don't know how to love.

And now I wonder: That fleeting, haunting comment that escaped Heather's lips one day like a bird surprised to find the cage door open—maybe that wasn't just my daughter speaking to me, but my Lord. A child's voice is the voice of God. This doesn't mean that everything a child says is what God would say, but the cry for love in a child's heart: This is God speaking to us.

Many parents are too busy for their children. Some Christians are so busy serving God that they have no time to love their children. But for every parent, the path to service lies through the hearts of our own children. If we do not give up our lives for our children, we will never do so for anyone else. Love begins at home.

To become childlike we must learn to love children. As long as my love for Heather was stingy and faltering, I could not enter into childlike faith. To become like a child I needed to love a child, purely and with wholehearted extravagance.

As a father my greatest frustration has been that this sort of love did not come to me naturally. I seemed to lack paternal instinct. But then, why should love come naturally? Love is not natural but supernatural. It comes from God, and if we don't have it, we must ask for it. What we don't know, we must learn.

Asking for love is what I was doing as I prayed that afternoon beside my sleeping daughter. For the next few years I'd be doing this more and more: praying for love. No, not even praying, but sitting mute as a stone at night waiting to be touched by a shaft of moonlight. For just as we do not know how to love, neither do we know how to pray for love. We really do not know anything at all about love. And here, in the humility of unknowing, is the place to start.

Some people do seem to love children naturally. Presumably these people will not need to read this book. But it is a great mistake to assume that all parents love their children. This myth rests upon a false concept of love.

If the myth were true, then how to account for all the sexual, physical, and emotional abuse that takes place in many families? Or what about the alienation, the cold formality, the lack of understanding that eats away at so many parent-child relationships? What about all those parents who have never even said the words "I love you," and so will never hear them back? What about all those children who, far from knowing they are the apple of someone's eye, go through life in the shadow of their parents' open disapproval or subtle, unspoken condemnation?

Once I was engaged in a spiritual discussion with a father. Out of the corner of his eye this man became aware that his young son, seated on the floor on the other side of the room, was sticking a finger up his nose. Suddenly a look of blind, undiluted rage swept over the father's face—like an expression one might see on a painted savage in the heat of jungle warfare—and he barked out a command that startled the poor child out of his wits.

Then, just as suddenly, the look of murderous rage vanished, and the man returned placidly to our adult conversation, as if there were no such thing in the world as poison arrows.

But I felt the jungle look was the true look, the one that said all there was to say about this man as a father. One look gave him away.

That day on the couch with Heather after story time, while the clouds floated by the window, my daughter's small, chance, piercing observation on my lovelessness touched off a gnawing, increasingly ravenous, years-long search in my life for love, for the real thing.

Strangely enough, I can point to the very day when my search came to an end—or at least, when I turned a decisive corner. It was a day in 1995 when I returned home full of excitement from a week-long absence. As my daughter ran into my arms to greet me, I lifted her up and swung her joyously in the air. Upon setting her down, I said, "Heather, look into my eyes. What do you see there?"

For a few moments Heather peered. And then her whole face broke into the loveliest smile as she sang out, "LOVE! I see LOVE!"

Heather, you saw correctly. Something had happened to me during my time away. I'd gone on a journey from my head to my heart, and I returned home, not only brimming with love, but with a deep resolve to keep that cup full. From this time on I saw the need to choose deliberately to let my daughter into my heart and to move toward her in love. Moreover, I saw that my love had to be unconditional.

There are some books whose titles alone speak volumes. One title I'll never forget is Raymond Carver's *What We Talk About When We Talk About Love.*

What are we talking about here? What is love?

Thankfully, we have an answer in 1 Corinthians 13:4-8:

Love is patient, love is kind. It does not envy, it does not boast, it is not proud. It is not rude, it is not self-seeking, it is not easily angered, it keeps no record of wrongs. Love does not delight in evil but rejoices with the truth. It always protects, always trusts, always hopes, always perseveres.

Love never fails.

To the above definition I would add the words of 1 John 2:10: "Whoever loves...lives in the light, and there is nothing in him to make him stumble."

Are you stumbling around as a parent? Do you grope in the darkness, worried sick because you cannot seem to help or even reach your children? If so, it's because you are not living in the light. If you were, you would not be stumbling.

This is a hard truth, but love must be unconditional. If we are stumbling, it is because we've attached conditions to our love. Remove the conditions, and we will know exactly what to do for our children.

You might wish to argue, "No, no, surely you're exaggerating. The love you are describing is too idealistic." To the extent that we believe this, we will settle for something less than unconditional love, and we will never go looking for the real thing.

The quality of our relationship with our children is the quality of our own life. That is, when someone asks us that dreaded question, "How are you?" the most honest answer we could give would be to describe our relationship with our children.

So: How are you? Perhaps you would have to admit, "My two-year-old daughter is tormenting my soul." Or, "I lie awake at night worried sick about my son." Or, "It would be easier to communicate with a rock at the bottom of the ocean than with my teenager."

Such statements would reveal the truth of how you are, not only in the parent-child relationship, but in every aspect of your life. If this sounds harsh, consider whether you don't judge yourself just as harshly. Doesn't the fact that you cannot manage a teenager, or even a two-year-old child, sit as a gnawing accusation at the center of your being?

Set your sights on pure, unconditional love and do not settle for anything less. Try believing in perfect love, seek it with all your heart, and it will find you.

Many times as Heather was growing up, I felt I had no relationship with her at all. It seemed as though everything I did for her or with her went through holes in a sieve, leaving no permanent result. Deep down, I felt terrified of the day when she would leave home and never come back. Or worse still, come back only to pay dutiful respects to a pair of old fossils.

Looking back on this period, I can see I was stuck in two quagmires: self-pity and self-condemnation. Both are diseases of unfulfilled love. Self-pity refuses to give love while self-condemnation refuses to accept love.

Self-pity, fixated on its own unfulfilled need for love, will not reach out and give love to anyone else. It doesn't understand that giving is receiving. If you want something, start giving it away and it will be yours. This principle holds true in all relationships, but especially between parents and children. I wanted my daughter's love and respect, but I would not offer these consistently to her.

Self-condemnation refuses to receive love. All love begins with the receiving of love. "This is love: not that we loved God, but that he loved us" (1 John 4:10). If we will not receive, we have nothing to give. Many parents fail because they are too proud to receive love from their children. They do not even love themselves, let alone accept love from anyone else.

Do you love yourself? Are you patient and gentle and kind with yourself? Do you easily let go of your mistakes and wrongs, or do you keep a strict record and punish yourself severely? Do you trust yourself enough to persevere always? Or are you continually doubting, berating, condemning yourself?

The way you treat yourself is the way you will treat your children.

I love to pray. It's my favorite thing to do. But the hardest lesson I've ever learned is that my life of prayer was not producing a life of love.

I became aware of this only because my family kept interrupting my prayers. Often this would happen just as I was enjoying some sense of revelation, some special touch from the Lord, an anointing, an ecstasy. I might pray for an hour and seem to get nowhere. Then, just when things got good, a little person would burst into the room shouting, "Daddy!"

Why would God give me times of special intimacy in prayer only to have them blown apart by intrusions? For years I puzzled and puzzled over this, until finally I learned this rule: First love, then pray.

Gradually I realized that whenever I felt God's presence it was always for the purpose of love. No wonder people kept interrupting my prayers! It's not the intrusions of people that spoil prayer. Rather, the refusal to love drives God away.

While our children may often appear whimsical and selfish, all they really want is our love. They want much more of our love than we are prepared to give. If we consistently practice giving love to children, eventually we'll no longer feel that they pull us away from God but only toward Him. The anointing of the Holy Spirit will come upon us to love, and in the midst of this love God's anointing will increase.

Step three of the Twelve-Step Program reads, "We made a decision to turn our will and our lives over to the care of God as we understood Him." As a parent I've often felt that the wording of this step might be changed. Or perhaps a step three and a half could be added that would read: "We made a decision to turn our will and our lives over to the care of God as we *did not* understand Him." Being a parent has a way of separating us from the God we understand and drawing us toward a God whom we cannot understand.

What does this feel like? It feels like getting up in the middle of the night to change a diaper and walk the floor. It feels like driving to Disneyland in ninety-degree heat with a car full of screaming kids spilling drinks and pulling each other's hair. It feels like giving your daughter a special present, only to have her throw a temper tantrum because it's not what she wanted. It feels like hearing your six-year-old swear at you, or your four-year-old say that you don't love her. And so on.

It can feel, in short, like being dragged through a knothole backward. It feels like being called on to give something when we have nothing to give. It feels the way Jesus' disciples must have felt when they came to Him worried that the crowd had no food, and He said, "You give them something to eat" (Matthew 14:16).

Love does not arise out of what we have to give, but out of knowing we have nothing to give. It is good to give what we have. But until we give what we have not, we fall short of unconditional love.

CHAPTER FOUR AND A HALF

# BUILDING BLOCKS

*Whoever welcomes this little child in my name welcomes me;*
*and whoever welcomes me welcomes the one who sent me.*
*For he who is least among you all—he is the greatest.*

LUKE 9:48

Throughout her early years Heather and I played with blocks.
Playtime on the living room floor was alien territory for me. I
hadn't played in years. It felt like trying to make an adjustment to
the core of a nuclear reactor. At seminary I'd taken Systematic Theology and Hermeneutics, but there was no course called Having
Fun.

Heather and I had two sets of blocks, one a standard collection
of cubes and oblongs, the other an intricate puzzle of odd-shaped
interlocking pieces that fit precisely into their own wooden box but
that, once apart, stayed apart forever. Both sets of blocks were
finely crafted with smooth, level sides that made them perfect for
building. The puzzle set I found especially satisfying, as it had the
half-moons, disks, and pyramids required for fine architectural
detail on castles.

Not that we made many castles at first. We built towers. I built tall towers, Heather built small towers. At least, I built mine as tall as I could manage, which wasn't very tall because Heather kept knocking them down.

Heather despised my tall towers because she couldn't get hers anywhere near as big. As for her small towers, who could be bothered with them? When building a tower you aim for the ceiling, right? Building tall towers was the only game I knew. At the time I failed to grasp how this fact mirrored my life.

Naturally Heather took outrageous delight in knocking down my towers. This angered me, and I couldn't understand why she kept on doing it. I didn't always show my anger, but usually, after a couple of crashes, I'd just lose interest in playing with blocks.

Tall or small: Which would it be? Build big and get knocked down, or stay small and have fun?

Eventually I had to learn to have fun. Then the game became guarding my tower while Heather fought desperately to get at it. These were real contests in which the sides were evenly matched: I was bigger and stronger, but the tower was fragile, Heather was more determined, and I was not allowed to hurt her. Most of the time she succeeded in breaking through my defenses. But sometimes if her play-desperation suddenly ignited into real desperation, I'd have to relent and let her win.

CRASH!

As time went on I became aware of a peculiar change in me. I was actually anticipating and enjoying the crashes as much as Heather did. This change did not happen overnight. When you've spent your life thinking the game was to build the tallest tower in town, it's odd having the rules suddenly altered.

In the final scene of the movie *Zorba the Greek,* a grand scheme of Zorba's crashes to ruin. He has come up with a method of conveying logs from a mountainside down to the beach where they can be easily transported by water. But as the first logs come rumbling down the brand-new chute, the whole colossal structure collapses thunderingly in a cloud of dust.

After a few sobering moments Zorba turns to his boss, the pragmatic, strait-laced man who has funded the project, and makes a comment I have never forgotten: "Boss, you've got everything except one thing: madness. A man needs a little madness or else he never cuts the rope to be free."

Then, there on the empty beach amidst the still-settling dust of their stupendous failure, the two men link arms and dance ecstatically.

Learning to love crashes was just one small building block in a different sort of tower that was being built in my heart—a castle of love. Like my wooden-block towers, this interior castle continually got knocked down. For the longest time, whenever this happened I knew only three reactions: rage, indifference, or despair.

It never occurred to me there was a fourth option: I could celebrate the crash, laugh like crazy over it, then clear away the wreckage and patiently begin again.

I believed, you see, that love is a fragile thing, easily destroyed.

I didn't yet know the real thing.

When Heather was a baby I recall reading something about "interpersonal congruency." The author defined this as a shared experience between two people that registers in the form of a matching expression on their faces.

For example, if someone feels downhearted and tells me a sad story, my face assumes the same sad expression as his. If I am truly listening and commiserating, a moment will come when the expressions on our two faces will be so parallel that it is like looking into an emotional mirror. In that moment, something passes between the two hearts and a bonding occurs. Many, many such experiences over time produce a close relationship.

On one level this idea seems patently obvious. But as a first-time father the notion of personal congruency struck a deep chord with me. When I felt lost in the jungle of fatherly love, this insight gave me a place to start.

One day as I was setting the last block atop a teetering tower, my big adult face and my daughter's tiny rose petal met in a look of precisely the same mischievous, wide-eyed thrill. In that moment a spark passed between us, and somehow it helped me to know that this event was not random and ephemeral but a solid building block of love.

Here was some very serious fun. Slaves are bound by chains, loved ones by strings of jewels made up of traded gleams in the eye, secret smiles, common struggles. The tower of wooden blocks would topple, but the tower of personal congruency, built patiently with enough golden moments, would hold firm.

For a long time I failed to understand the foolishness of expecting a consistent quality of relationship from a child. As mature adults we value consistency. We like people to "be there," to exhibit certain standards of loyalty and of friendly (or at least polite) behavior. In our minds, predictability spells dependability.

But to a child, predictability may be boring. If you paid good money for a roller-coaster ride, wouldn't you get edgy if it turned out smooth? From one day to the next, children are changing and growing. The only life they know is a roller-coaster ride. Children are always experimenting with who they are and with how much they can squeeze out of life; they're always leaving one child behind to go in quest of another.

It is dangerous to count on having normal, healthy relationships with people who do not know who they are and may not particularly care. If their own identity is in wild fluctuation, the same will be true of their relationships.

Therefore abandon all expectations for a mature friendship with the immature. In place of consistency, look for beautiful moments, and take full advantage of these as they're offered. In parenting, as in mountain climbing, we rarely see the peak while climbing. Be ready for the awesome glimpses of intimacy that children will offer you, and for the rest, plod on.

In the relationship between God and His people, God is male and people are female. Jesus is our lover and we are His bride. Similarly in the parent-child relationship, parents represent the man and children the woman. In practice this means that children need to be wooed, chased, and won.

A friend told me that he once chased his tiny daughter down the hall yelling savagely, "I love you, I love you, I want to turtle-dove you!" As he swept her into his arms, he had a sudden insight into the passionate, all-encompassing, energetically pursuing, and romancing love of God the Father.

Children need to be romanced. When a girl grows up to be a woman, she may find love with a man her own age. But as a little girl she can find true love only with a person much older, an adult. Though too young for romantic love and sex, she craves something that feels as good.

Story times, playtimes, cuddling, tête-à-têtes—these are all part of the peculiar language of romance between parents and children. On the outside this picture looks quite different than that between a man and a woman in love. But inside it should feel almost the same. It should feel at least as good.

Indeed there's a chance it will feel even better, because in this relationship one person (the adult) has some idea of what to do. This factor ought to eliminate much of the nonsense in grown-up romances.

If the love between a father and his daughter does not feel at least as exquisite as grown-up love, then when the little girl matures she will not know what to look for in a man. If the necessary code for true romantic love has not been imprinted on her heart, she may end up being seduced by something false.

Naturally both parents need to impart this romantic code to their sons and daughters. For in a sense there are three genders of humanity: male, female and child. To a child every adult is like a person of the opposite sex.

As children grow older and relationships mature, the mystery of interpersonal congruency becomes more complex. A shared smile or a laugh here and there no longer satisfies. One must assemble broad networks of mutual experience.

In grade two Heather was still having trouble learning to read. Eventually we enrolled her in a remedial course called Aspire. At first she wanted none of this. She didn't like being singled out as a slow reader who needed special assistance. However, as I've always been a painfully slow reader myself, I decided to join her. This made it okay.

So one summer Dad and Heather headed downtown every morning to a tiny, cluttered room for reading school. Here the walls were covered with signs such as, "Few people understand the courage it takes for a child to return to a place where he failed yesterday and the day before and will probably fail again."

In this room Heather and I together did a bunch of crazy things that on the surface had nothing to do with reading. The instructor assured us that these activities would forge new pathways in the language centers of our brains.

For example, here I learned how to look at three-dimensional pictures—those that appear as flat geometrical designs until you refocus your eyes to a point above the page to bring the hidden picture to life. We also practiced balancing in sock feet on a rocking platform called the Belgau Board while performing various stunts with a ball attached to a string.

Through such exercises I cannot honestly say that I learned to read any better, but I did learn to see the world differently, and I also had a lot of fun with my daughter. As for her, on her young brain the treatment worked like a charm, and she's been reading voraciously ever since.

Let's move the clock forward. Heather is ten, it's a Sunday afternoon, and she and I carry a pile of sports equipment up to the park near our house. We've got a bat and ball, a Frisbee, a basketball, tennis and badminton rackets, and an old red Australian football that I love. At this age, rather than staying with one activity, Heather likes to sample a bit of everything.

My Australian football won't hold much air anymore, so it's soft enough not to knock Heather's head off. She still lacks confidence when it comes to catching or throwing balls. For years she wouldn't touch the football, but now we're tossing it around and she's doing pretty well. Every time she catches it, she looks surprised, as if the ball had come to her because it liked her.

After a while we make up some simple plays. I hike to her, drop back for a handoff, then she goes for a short pass or rolls out to the side for a lateral. We do fakes, zigzags, buttonhooks. My favorite play, of course, is the Long Bomb. But I know she's not ready for that.

Even so, just for fun, as we're in the huddle with our arms draped around each other's shoulders, I say, "Okay, Heath, it's time for the Long Bomb."

"The what?"

"The Long Bomb. You hike to me, then run like a jackrabbit as far as you can go. Don't look back until you hear me yell, then turn around and put up your arms, and the ball will be right there."

"How far should I go?"

"Far. Farther than you can believe. And don't worry. When I yell, you turn around and the ball will just be sitting there in the air like it's on a shelf just above your ear. All you have to do is reach up and nab it."

So Heather snaps the ball and starts loping out down the long field. How far should I let her go? I'm not even sure how far I can throw this thing anymore. But I feel the sweet, smooth adrenaline flowing into my arm and out to my fingertips, and I sense the same gorgeous stuff coursing through my daughter too, connecting us by an invisible cord as we both imagine her with fingers of sand-paper and arms that can reach out and encircle any star.

Once, just once, she looks back, wondering if I still exist, not believing I could possibly mean this far. But I yell, "No, no—not yet—keep on going—way down there—way-y-y-y-y-y dowwwwwwwwn there..."

So she keeps on going until finally something tells me, some mysterious signal, that this is it, this is the moment, and I lean back against the wind, one arm stretched forward and one way back, front toe barely touching the ground, and then I let fly that soaring star, launch it like a missile and can almost hear it whistling through the air, homing to its mark, while in my bones I'm wanting, wishing, willing my daughter to catch it, picturing it live and kicking in her hands, a red leather bomb still moving like fury but yielding to her if only she'll tighten her grip around it like a cat's jaws into a bird's throat until she has it, has it for ever and ever, bringing it tight against her body until no one can take it away from her, no one can ever take that moment away.

And that's when I yell: "OKAY, HEATHER!" And as she turns around, sure enough the ball is right there, right on the money, hanging beside her ear like an apple that, as she reaches for it, seems to turn into a bird and float right into her hands. And then she has it. Tight against her body. For ever and ever. YES!

For a moment, bewildered, she looks back at me in disbelief, peers back at the tiny figure of her father way down at the other end of the field, such a long, long distance away. And then she explodes. She jumps straight up in the air and cheers and then starts running toward me, and I run toward her, and we're both running and jumping and yelling with all the joy that's fountaining up from deep inside us into our throats and mouths and spilling out all over that great gigantic field.

My daughter, ten years old, has just caught the longest pass her old man can throw, and as we rush into each other's arms, the field, the whole earth, moves under our feet, spins with love.

# CHAPTER FIVE

# LIVING STORIES

*Jesus spoke all these things to the crowd in parables;*
*he did not say anything to them without using a parable.*

MATTHEW 13:34

For eighteen years I went to school without a break. By the time I graduated with a master's in English, I was tired of the whole business. Fed up with formal education, I wanted to get out into the world and do some real living.

I'll never forget the feeling of freedom when, a week after finishing my final exam, I entered a library merely to browse. Never again would I *have* to read anything. From now on I was free to read only what I wanted, when I wanted. I could finish a book or not, as I chose. I could give up reading altogether. Leaving school revolutionized my reading life, and a new life opened up to me.

A similar revolution took place when I started reading storybooks with my daughter. Now, once again, with the time constraints upon a parent's life, I was not free to read whatever and whenever I liked. Instead I discovered a new luxury: the joy of reading aloud to a child.

We've never had a TV in our home and Heather has never asked for one, but she has continually asked for stories. She and I would disappear into the library and bring home piles, armloads of picture books. We'd take out forty or fifty books at a crack and that would do us a week.

What a time we had! What treasures lay in those books! And the pictures! No pictures are more delicious than the illustrations in children's books. To my mind the world's greatest art lies hidden in children's literature.

By this point in my life I had, without wanting to admit it, grown tired of reading. To a reader this is tragic, like going blind. But reading aloud with Heather renewed my love of books. As children's stories worked their magic on me, I realized that for forty years I'd been living an unillustrated life. Even the poorer, disappointing picture books somehow gave me greater pleasure than long adult novels. This was partly because of their smallness. Like children themselves, they didn't beat around the bush but came to their small point quickly. Each slender volume contained a whole new world of discovery. It was just as if the fairies were standing on the edge of the page and beckoning me into their enchanting realm.

Heather's first Bible was a fast-paced children's version with simple text and pictures on every page. It covered most of the best-known stories in both testaments, but Heather's favorite was the Crucifixion. When she wanted to hear this story, Heather would say,

"Daddy, I want Jesus died." How often I heard these words as she climbed up on the couch beside me, clutching her fat little Bible. Then we'd turn to the picture of Jesus alone in the garden and to the one on the next page with the three dark crosses on a hill, and we would read the few simple words there.

Heather never tired of this story. In our home there must be two dozen different children's versions of the Christmas story, all of which Heather has enjoyed. But her fixation with the cross has run deeper. Somehow my little girl knew intuitively that the cross is the most important thing in the whole universe. And it wasn't just the cross itself that fascinated her, but the actual blood of Jesus. She could never get her fill of His blood.

Although her Bible was the best version for young children we could find, I have one criticism of it. While the original Gospels devote a huge and disproportionate amount of space to the Passion and Crucifixion, Heather's Bible covered these in a couple of pages. And the description of Jesus' death was not at all explicit: no nails, no blood, no violence. The picture showed the crosses as shadowy silhouettes and the words said merely, "So they killed Him on a cross. It was a sad day for Jesus' friends."

Before becoming a father I might have designed a children's Bible this way. But not now. With Heather it was always, "I want Jesus died," and she wanted all the gory details too. She and I used to look at books of paintings of the life of Jesus, and there again it was always, "Daddy, I want Jesus died." She wanted to see the rough wood and the ugly nails and the dripping blood, and at such times she would be full of a holy solemnity.

Delicate parents may be disturbed by the violence of children's play. Boys especially love war games, cops and robbers, cowboys and Indians. But violence for its own sake is not what these games are about. Rather, like the Crucifixion, they are about the war between good and evil.

To children this war is very real. Adults have found ways to insulate themselves from the war and to pretend that it does not exist. But to children the battle is obvious and ever present. War is so real to children that they must continually rehearse their part in it through stories and imaginary play.

Girls have their own ways of dramatizing the invisible. Once, when Heather was five, I overheard her and a friend conspiring to play what may be the world's favorite children's game: "Pretend you're the prince and I'm the princess and we're living together and our mother and father are dead and we can do anything we want."

Was I shocked to be the dead father in this game? Not at all, because a short while later I sat cozily with Heather on the couch reading a storybook filled with princesses, goblins, and war.

Good stories, like life itself, have an integrity that cannot be censored. Cut out the bad from a story and you damage its heart. According to Paul, "It is shameful even to mention what the disobedient do in secret" (Ephesians 5:12), yet the Bible itself is full of tales of the secret doings of the wicked. Paul, of course, was warning against gossip, and literature is not gossip. Stories provide one of the few healthy contexts in which it is possible, even necessary, to speak the unspeakable. Stories tell all in a way that mirrors and prepares for the no-holds-barred onslaught of real life. This is the root of the therapeutic power of stories. Tales are the salve of the healer.

Not only did Jesus' preaching rely heavily on stories, but in His ministry He moved increasingly from telling stories to enacting them. He rode a donkey into Jerusalem, cursed a fig tree, washed His disciples' feet. Large portions of the Gospels consist of parables, fictional stories that Jesus presumably made up. But the greatest parable, the one that comprises the final third of each gospel, is a true one. It's a story full of the blood and violence that children respond to so readily.

A child's life may seem simpler than that of an adult, but it is still a moral life. Children make moral choices of their own from the time of conception. If babies are born in sin, then babies can also respond to the gospel and be saved. As David wrote, "You made me trust in you even at my mother's breast" (Psalm 22:9). If a mere infant can trust in God, then perhaps faith is something different than we thought.

When the pregnant Elizabeth was visited by the pregnant Mary, "the baby leaped in her womb, and Elizabeth was filled with the Holy Spirit" (Luke 1:41). This jumper-for-joy was none other than John the Baptist—the first human being to recognize and worship the Christ. How humbling to think that a fetus might have more faith than many an adult. Since an infant can know God, which is all there is to know, in a mysterious way the child whose life is tragically snuffed out has lived as fully as the octogenarian.

No wonder most good children's stories, and all fairy tales,

contain a full range of emotions including a healthy dose of violence and the grotesque. Children need this in order for the real
world to be convincingly reflected to them. Children find themselves in stories in a way that many people never find themselves in
real life. The story, while it may contain all the tensions and dan-
gers of the world at large, is safe.

In Jesus' day there was no Christian theology. There were only stories. There were only events and experiences and witnesses of those
things, only that "which we have heard, which we have seen with
our eyes, which we have looked at and our hands have touched"
(1 John 1:1).

By the middle of the first century Paul would be theologizing.
He would make sense of the stories. But in its essence the gospel is
not theology but pure story. Certain things happened for which
there was no immediate explanation. The first Christians were not
explainers or theologians, they were simply witnesses.

Being childlike involves loosening our hold on explanation and
returning to the humble status of witness. It means letting go of
trying to manipulate events and instead, like a child on his father's
knee, becoming captivated by the story of our lives.

This is always how it is with the gospel. The gospel is good
news, and news is current events, a story that unfolds in the present. Whenever the kingdom of heaven makes advances, whether in

the first or in the twenty-first century, there is no explaining it. There is only the witness of people carried along in the flow of God's stupendous action in history.

Later it will all be explained, analyzed, codified, pigeon-holed. But at the time it is happening, it is just happening. Happening to *me!* It is too big, too sweeping, too entrancing to explain. It is like being caught up in a page-turner of a novel in which you really do not know what is going to happen next or why.

Children live this way. Children and stories are inseparable because children live stories. Adults tend to live in their heads, relentlessly analyzing. But children experience life directly. To children life is a story in which they are the main character.

Adults, not content simply to be characters, want to be the author of their story. Being part of a story means surrendering control, but we like to think we can control our world, or at least a good chunk of it. At the very least we'd like to control our children!

Children know (at least better than adults) that they have little control. They have tantrums because they do not even bother trying to control themselves. They know they are not in control of their story, that they are not the author. To a greater or lesser extent, life simply unfolds for them. Only gradually do they enter into the state of self-realization wherein their actions become more conscious and deliberate.

To be a little child is to believe implicitly in good and evil, in heroes and villains, in the invisible, in miracles and mystery, in princesses and dragons, in true love and in happy endings. To be a child is to be caught up in pure story, embracing the events of one's life uncritically because one trusts the Author.

This is what happened to the apostle John in writing the book of Revelation. Of the four gospels John's is the latest and so contains the most theology. By the time he wrote it, John had done a good deal of thinking about the events he had witnessed, and this shows in the writing.

Later in life, however, when John was exiled to the island of Patmos, once again he was caught up in pure story and he became a mere witness. With his rational faculties overwhelmed, before his eyes cataclysmic events unfolded in the heavenly realms. He did not analyze these; he only wrote them down. He was told, "Write…what you have seen" (Revelation 1:19) not "Write what you think."

Theologians still argue over how to think about the story John told in Revelation. Like all great stories, this book defies analysis. Seen and written through childlike eyes, its code cannot be broken by the rational mind.

Similarly, when I became a Christian, it was not by means of rational analysis but rather by falling on my knees and giving my life to Christ in an act that was beyond my comprehension. I did not choose Christ, He chose me. All I did was respond to His amazing call and presence. I was caught up in a story with a spellbinding hero. In that moment I relinquished control of my personal history and became a character in His story. I became a child once more, born again.

This is not a one-time event but one that keeps on happening in my spiritual life. The New Testament teaches not only that I'm saved but that I'm in a process of "being saved" (1 Corinthians 1:18). All of us should experience theology being continually yanked out of our grasp and turned back into pure story. For the kingdom of heaven is today's news.

# A PLACE CALLED HOPE

*She is a tree of life to those who embrace her;*
*those who lay hold of her will be blessed.*

PROVERBS 3:18

Having talked enough about stories in the last chapter, now let's tell one. What follows is a true story about my daughter Heather. I wrote it in her voice as if she were telling it, and it goes like this...

When I was five years old, my family moved away from a place called Hope. That really was its name.

Hope was a little town nestled in the mountains, and our house was right beside a crystal-clear rushing river. Everything about Hope was like that: beautiful.

I had a best friend, Janelle, just two doors away. Janelle was the sort of friend who always wanted to play exactly what you wanted to play. I guess we must have had some fights too. But that's not what I remember.

Hope had everything you could want. Our house was on a quiet crescent, hardly any cars on the street. In the middle of the crescent was a big park, half woods and half open field. The field had lots of flowers, and it felt as if you could run in it forever. The woods were threaded with paths, and every tree was special.

The day the moving truck came, my dad told me that once all the furniture was out, I could go inside one last time and say good-bye to the empty house. That sounded so important. But at the last minute things got too busy. The moving truck was already leaving, and my dad said we had to leave ahead of it to meet the movers at the new place. Everything was happening in a rush; it felt like the whole of my life was slipping away in one gulp. I cried and cried, but it didn't help.

I never did get to say good-bye to my room. To this day I cannot imagine what my room would have looked like without anything in it.

Everything about the move was like that: awful. We moved to the city, to a place called Langley. In Hope we had a beautiful house; in Langley we had an awful apartment. It was small, dark, dingy. Hardly any children lived there. There was one girl my age, Erica, but she was awful. My parents kept encouraging me to play with her. But she was really too much, even for them. She was always pounding on our piano. The first time she saw it, she said, "How do you turn this thing on?" She had never even seen a piano before! After that, we couldn't keep her away from it.

Because the apartment was so much smaller than our house, we had to put a lot of our stuff in storage. All kinds of things disappeared, and some of them I never saw again. In Hope I had a favorite little wooden rocking chair, and one day my dad finally confessed that he had sold it to a secondhand store. Without even telling me!

Langley had no woods. When we lived in Hope, I was only five, not yet old enough to play in the woods alone. But when we moved, I kept thinking about all those paths through the trees and what fun it would be to play there. How I'd looked forward to that! But now it would never happen.

On top of everything else, we almost lost our cat, Molly. In the new neighborhood a mean tom terrorized her, and the two times we let her out, she didn't come back. We were lucky to find her, and after that she had to learn to stay inside.

Over and over my parents told me why we had moved to this awful place. But it never made any sense to me. Why would anyone leave paradise to move to a hole in the wall?

My parents told me that the school in Langley would be much better than the school in Hope. We moved in the summertime, just before I started kindergarten, so I didn't know much about school yet, but I could not believe that there could really be anything wrong with the school in Hope. Why would there be? In Hope there was nothing wrong with anything. Hope was perfect in every way.

After about a year in the apartment, we moved to a bigger place, a townhouse with woods nearby. Next door there lived a girl my age, Alisa, and we became great friends. Now I knew another person who wanted to play exactly what I wanted to play. We played Laura and Mary (from the *Little House on the Prairie* books) or Pony Pals, or we played being animals in the woods (deer and raccoons were our favorites), or sometimes we played games of terror (like pretending our parents had died). Alisa and I thought the same way about things, and our ideas always fit together.

The only problem was that Alisa had other friends besides me, and I could never quite figure out whether I was her best friend. Sometimes she was available to be my best friend, and sometimes not. Later this got sorted out, but in the beginning it kept me pretty confused.

Alisa and I went to the same school, the city school that was supposed to be so great. It was okay. The best thing about it, I always thought, was recess.

One recess in kindergarten, Alisa and I were inspecting all the trees in the schoolyard, looking over the possibilities for play. To our surprise, we found one tree that was (still is) different from all the others. This tree is absolutely unique. The bark is this lovely, pale, pinkish white. Not pure white, like paper, but white for a tree. White the way people say my skin is white. And smooth, almost satiny. If you rub against it, some of the white stuff comes off on you.

I don't know for sure what kind of tree this is. Not a birch, I know that. Maybe a poplar, maybe a dogwood. I've heard that Jesus' cross was made of dogwood. Anyway, from the very first this tree fascinated Alisa and me, and we decided to name her. We called her Pransanna. (Or maybe it's Prance-a-nah, or something like that. Since we never wrote it down, I don't really know how to spell it.) How we came up with this name, I'm not sure. I think Alisa said something about a prince, and I said something about a princess, and somehow prancing horses got involved, and the name that came out was Pransanna.

It's an odd name. The more I think about it, the odder it seems. Odd too that Alisa and I should have thought it up. I think, frankly, that Pransanna must really be the tree's name. Not a made-up name, but her real one. I think she must have told it to us, whispered it to us from her dancing leaves.

Pransanna's leaves are like a golden snowfall. At least, they're like that in fall, when I first met her. In winter she becomes a tall, stately lady, and in spring she is a shimmering green sun. She has many moods, and many mysteries.

One mystery about Pransanna is that she's crowded right up against another tree, an evergreen, just inches away. Neat rows of evenly spaced evergreens line the whole play field. And then there's Pransanna, the only tree of her kind, the only one to break the pattern. How did this happen? Who left her to grow there, and why? Did someone take a shine to her, some principal or janitor? Or does Pransanna have a way of making herself invisible to adults?

Here's another mystery: Pransanna has a heart carved into her trunk. It's quite faded now, overgrown with new bark; it must have been carved a long time ago. Inside the heart is a letter, just one letter. It has the shape of an L, but backward, with the bottom stroke pointing left. Perhaps some kid was cutting initials inside a heart, when suddenly the school bell rang and that was the end of it. The kid never came back to finish his work.

But I have a different theory. My guess is that Pransanna made the heart herself and put the letter inside it. That's why the L is turned backward, because Pransanna wrote it herself from the inside.

I also think I know what the L stands for.

Every recess Alisa and I would have races to Pransanna on the far side of the play field. The moment the bell rang, we'd be out the door in a flash and running for all we were worth across that field to get to Pransanna. Alisa was a faster runner, but I was faster getting out and was often there first. As soon as I reached Pransanna, I'd throw my arms around her. She has the loveliest curve to her trunk, so lithe and lively, just the right shape for hugging, and taking her in your arms and feeling the give in her, you twirl around her and then slide down, still holding tight to her waist but leaning way back till you're almost on the ground and gazing up into her shining hair, just like swinging a partner on the dance floor. I have done this, this exact move, hundreds of times.

Alisa and I had all sorts of games we played with and around Pransanna. The line that marked the edge of the field ran right beside her, and we pretended that this was a deep crack in the earth. You can imagine all the games that came out of that! Or often we played house and Pransanna was our cupboard, or a door, or whatever we needed her to be. Other times we played that she was the Queen of All the Trees.

Sometimes, however, I had to play alone. Alisa had other

friends at school, friends who weren't like her. They never wanted to play what I wanted to play, and they didn't know about Pransanna.

Whenever Alisa got involved with her other friends and I felt left out, I would go to Pransanna for comfort. I cried many tears into her soft, white bark. She was my best friend of all. You might say she was my best-friend-rooted-to-the-ground. For really, I came to see, there is no one, no one person, who is always going to want exactly what you want. Only Pransanna. I could always depend on her. She knew me through and through. In fact, I felt she knew everything there was to know—all about love and joy, and where pain and hatred came from. I could talk to Pransanna about anything and she would understand. She is the greatest thing I have ever seen face to face. I knew that she would never, ever leave me.

What I hadn't counted on was the possibility of my leaving her. But this is how it turned out. In fact, one day my whole school moved away from Pransanna.

What happened was that my school joined with another one. Since both schools were old and small, we moved together into a brand-new building. Changes, changes, always changes. In Hope I lived beside a river, on solid ground. Ever since then, it seems, I've been in the river, or the river's been in me.

The year my school moved I was eight years old. On the last day of classes, I said good-bye to Pransanna and I promised to come back and visit her. I said I would come whenever I could, but I especially promised to visit her on my ninth birthday, March 28, 1996.

Now I am nine. My birthday was a couple of weeks ago. It was a good day, but busy, and somehow the visit with Pransanna got missed. I asked my mom to take me, but I don't think she heard or understood. She said we had far too much to do to think about visiting trees.

The other day I was with my dad in the car when we passed the old school. Suddenly it all came over me, how much Pransanna meant to me. I asked Daddy if we could please stop and look around the old playground. He said no, we had far too much to do.

And then I burst into tears.

"Oh, all right," he said. "But only for ten minutes. Not a minute more."

Ten minutes was fine with me. That was almost as long as a recess. When we got onto the play field, I ran like the wind, just like I used to, ran with all my might to get to Pransanna. And I grabbed hold of her and swung her around, or she swung me around, and the sky moved above us. She felt just the same, so smooth and lovely and solid and giving. I was so happy to see her! That week I was learning to do cartwheels, real ones, so I did some for Pransanna, just to show her.

"Heather," said my dad, "isn't that grass pretty wet for rolling around on?"

"Who cares?" I yelled, bursting with joy.

Later, back home in bed, as my dad was saying good night to me, I told him all about Pransanna. I could feel my dad getting very quiet. There's a quietness of not talking, but there's another, deeper kind of quietness—a quietness of listening. The quietness that trees have. That's how quiet my dad got as I was telling him about Pransanna.

"Daddy," I said eventually. "Will Pransanna always be there? Even when I'm all grown up?"

My dad looked at me for a long, long time before answering.

"Yes, Heather," he said finally. "There will always be a Pransanna."

CHAPTER SIX

# LULLABIES FOR THE SOUL

*My heart is not proud, O LORD,*
*my eyes are not haughty;*
*I do not concern myself with great matters*
*or things too wonderful for me.*
*But I have stilled and quieted my soul;*
*like a weaned child with its mother,*
*like a weaned child is my soul within me.*

PSALM 131:1-2

One morning as I sat down for my quiet time, feeling dull and heavy, I was anticipating a long session of prayer in order to work my way out of this hole. I happened to be sitting beside a bookshelf filled with picture books of Heather's, mostly ones we hadn't read for a long time. On impulse I picked one off the shelf that I couldn't remember seeing before. Entitled *The Child's Book of Psalms,* it was a short selection of well-known psalm verses illustrated with simple line drawings.

It was a decidedly plain book, homely and unattractive. Why I was drawn to it I do not know. But as I opened it and began to read, something happened. Immediately my dull mood was transformed to one of lightness, wonder, joy and praise. The change was so sudden and sweeping that I knew beyond question it was the Lord's hand alone and no virtue of mine that had rescued me from the pit.

The portions of Psalms quoted in the book were old standards that I knew well. Yet as I read these familiar verses, they leaped to life. The words seemed filled with tremendous goodness and pure light.

When I read, "Thou anointest my head with oil; my cup runneth over," I literally felt warmth and love flowing all through my body.

When I read, "O send out thy light and thy truth: let them lead me," I felt literally bathed in an otherworldly light that I knew could never fade away but would grow brighter and brighter.

When I read, "He shall cover thee with his feathers, and under his wings shalt thou trust," I suddenly felt trust as something so real that I could actually touch and feel it on my skin.

When I read, "Praise him, all ye stars of light," I felt like a little child lying on my back on a hillside and beholding the stars as if for the first time.

In a few moments that small book transformed my view of the Bible—and of the world. Not since I had first accepted Scripture as God's Word had I experienced such a foundational shift in my understanding. Something like cobwebs fell from my eyes; layers of dust were swept from the coils of my brain. My twentieth-century skepticism collapsed like a house of cards, as if it were the quaintest and most absurd of antiquated sophistries. I felt like some new kind of being, a sort of amalgam of adult and child, having an adult's consciousness but a child's vivid senses, unquestioning trust, and limitless imagination.

Like a character in a children's fantasy, in a trice I was translated back from modern times into the world of the Bible, a childlike world closer to Eden, a world in which the power and majesty of the Creator God were beyond question. A veil had been removed from reality, the dull coating of civilized rationalism had been scraped away so that the true world, the one obviously spelled into being by an awesome God, could shine through.

If I had to pick one word to encapsulate this change, it would be *wonder*. Suddenly the Bible seemed a wondrous book full of marvelous words for banishing all evil. Suddenly the world it described was a shining, mystical world, the home not of malls and newspapers and automobiles but of angels, beautiful gardens, and rivers of living water. There were enemies, yes, and darkness and pitfalls, but so pure and radiant was the power in this book that every obstacle could be readily overcome with a word, with a song, or with some secret weapon.

Reading *The Child's Book of Psalms* was like sitting in a waiting room at the dentist's office and looking at a photograph of a clear mountain stream, when all at once the water begins to move, the pebbles in the bottom shine like jewels, and a dreamlike fawn comes down to drink. What treasures lay in this slim volume! For weeks afterward I would sit down to pray, not with the Bible beside me, but with *The Child's Book of Psalms.* Often I didn't even have to open it. One glance at the cover was enough to recall all the sights, the sounds, the scents, the feel of living in a realm of wonders under the loving protection of an all-wise, all-powerful Father God.

Through this homely book, not only Psalms but all of Scripture came alive for me. Psalms had always been my favorite book, the one I turned to most often, especially in times of trouble when I needed guidance and comforting. But now I saw that just as for children Mother Goose rhymes form the introduction to literature, so the psalms are the key to all the rest of the Bible. They are the Bible's prayer book, and prayer is the doorway to understanding Scripture.

Psalm 131, quoted at the head of this chapter, is the one that best conveys the childlike spirit. Yet doesn't every psalm possess this same essential character and move in this same direction? They are all songs of littleness, about becoming little and resting in the arms of our great and loving Father. The psalms are poems and hums for little people, the lullabies of the soul sung by Mother Spirit to the restless flesh.

The psalms usher adult minds into the world of children. In this book God Himself, like a little boy at play, "stretches out the heavens like a tent" and "makes the clouds his chariot" (104:2-3). Here is a world in which "rivers clap their hands" (98:8), mountains skip "like rams, the hill like lambs" (114:4), and "all the trees of the forest will sing for joy" (96:12). Here both praises and curses,

rather than being censored by our rational minds, are spontaneously uttered. This is a world in which enemies are real.

Many people today do not even realize they have enemies, and
so they do not know what to make of all the grisly, warlike verses in
Psalms. But children can feel when an enemy is breathing down
their necks, and like a child the psalmist honestly says what he
feels. If he's angry at his enemies he shouts, "Rise up, O LORD, confront them, bring them down" (17:13). If he's happy and thankful,
he just blurts it out. The psalmist cannot contain himself. Like a
toddler he runs up and throws his arms around his Daddy and
sings out, "I love you!"

Herein lies the great healing power of these divine poems.
Instead of bottling things up inside, the psalms tell it like it is. They
are like children who have nothing to hide. Of all the frank and
powerful emotions displayed in the psalms, the greatest is their
expression of wonder and worship—worship of God and wonder
at His works:

> Come and see what God has done,
>> how awesome his works in man's behalf! (66:5)
> Praise the LORD, O my soul;
>> all my inmost being, praise his holy name. (103:1)

As simple as these words are, there is something inim-
itable about them. Though I've read several modern attempts at the
writing of psalms, they aren't the same. They are never quite so

extravagant or abandoned as the originals. They don't go on and on. Rather than spilling over the top, they stop short, suddenly shy and self-conscious, as if aware of how ridiculous their words must sound, how foolish it is to imagine an invisible, all-powerful Friend.

While many believers have regular experiences of spontaneous praise and wonder, how hard it is to express these in words! Is this because our wonder tends to be fleeting rather than an ingrained habit of soul? Why not live, as Rabbi Abraham Heschel exhorted, with an attitude of "radical amazement"? He wrote, "Awareness of the divine begins with wonder.... What we lack is not a will to believe but a will to wonder."[3]

Sometimes I'll look at a tree, or at a cloud or a stream, and I'll think, "This is enough. If nothing else happened in my life except that I saw this one beautiful thing, still I would be compelled to fall on my face in worship of my awesome Creator. Just to have seen this, just to know this one moment, is far beyond anything I could have dreamed."

One day Heather said to me, "I used to think that things just happened in the world. I know it snows a lot in some places and it doesn't snow much here, but I thought that was just the way it was. I didn't know there was any reason for it, except that God made it that way. I didn't know that the reason we don't get much snow is we're close to the ocean, which has a warming influence because water loses heat more slowly than land, and so on. I just thought God decided it would snow a lot in some places but not much here, and so that's the way it was.

"And you know," she continued, "I still think that way, really. I think all the scientific reasons I've been learning in school really don't explain very much. I think things just are the way they are."

What a profound insight! David says the same in Psalm 65:9: "The streams of God are filled with water...for so you have ordained it."

Heather's talk of snow reminded me of a story about my brother Jimmie. I never knew Jimmie because he died at the age of three, before I was born. But my mother told me that one day shortly before his death Jimmie was looking out a window and watching the snow fall. All at once he said, "Mommy, the snow is good. God sends the snow."

Can't you just hear a small boy making this statement in that matter-of-fact tone children have when commenting on miracles?

Another time Jimmie was watching his electric train go round and round. In that same tone of frank wonder he said, "Look, Mommy—God makes it go!"

Who's right—Jimmie or the scientists? Does God make things go, or is it electricity?

When I told these two stories about Jimmie to Heather, without batting an eye she responded, "Jimmie's right. I think he was an angel sent from heaven to teach your family about God. When his time was up, he went back home."

Children live in a different world than adults do. It's a

prescientific world in which the rules and explanations are simple and self-evident. Children live in the book of Psalms.

As a four-year-old I believed I could do anything. One of my early memories is of debating this fact with an older friend. I can still see the two of us standing at the end of my driveway as I stated confidently, "Oh yes, I can do anything."

"Can you touch a cloud?" he challenged.

Not knowing that this feat could be accomplished easily on a foggy day, I replied instead, "No, I can't do that. But God can."

My friend stared at me blankly. What kind of an answer was this? Its brilliant illogicality was lost upon his older mind. Yet in the conceptual world of a child, I had uttered a wise and satisfying response.

Did the sun rise this morning? Answer yes or no.

The correct answer, of course, is no. Any fool knows that the sun does not rise, but rather the earth rises and sets while the sun, relatively speaking, remains stationary. Nevertheless in response to this question most people would say, "Yes, the sun rose this morning." So there are ways in which even as adults we continue to inhabit a child's world.

We think we know so much, when really we know so little. Isn't this what's delightful about small children? It's fun being around people who don't know much because everything is new to them. Secretly wouldn't we all like to be back there, back in the days when everything was new, always and continually?

You stale married couples—what if you could return to the time when you first fell in love, first kissed, first sat around gazing googly-eyed at each other and talking a blue streak? What would it be worth to you to feel those feelings again? Trouble is, after ten or twenty years together, you think you know each other. Really your "knowledge" is nothing but a load of misconceptions. If you truly knew, you would not be bored.

The psalms, if we let them, have the capacity to restore us to a world of wonders, to the first blush of our original love affair with life and its Maker. Just to be alive for one day on this planet is already to be as rich and lucky and loved as it is possible to be, and everything is more mysterious and wonderful than anyone can say or even think.

An old man smiles.

A young girl stares.

A child walks home from school through a back lane in the gathering twilight.

Mist flows like the robes of God through the streets of the town.

Snow falls, silent and glistening, sweet as new grass.

The sun goes down.

Birds fly.

Sounds drift from far away.

It rains.

In the first light of morning I sit on my porch and I cannot imagine how it is possible for me to experience all of these wonders within myself.

And yet I do.

# GARDEN FRESHNESS

*See that you do not look down on one of these little ones.*
*For I tell you that their angels in heaven*
*always see the face of my Father in heaven.*

MATTHEW 18:10

"I hate Eve," said Heather one day.

We were sitting in a restaurant, sipping hot chocolate.

"Eve? Eve who?" I asked, bewildered.

"You know—Eve in the Bible," Heather answered. "I hate her.
She was so stupid."

"You mean, to take the apple?"

"Yeah. That was so dumb. If she hadn't done that, the world
wouldn't be such an awful place."

"But don't you think that you might have done the same
thing?"

"No way!" she shot back. "I would never have done that."

"But Heather," I suggested gently, "you do things like that
every day."

"Only because of her," she retorted. "Why do I have to suffer
because of her? Why didn't God just make everyone good?"

At this point in the conversation I had to pause and think. This question still bothers me, even though I have an answer for it. It's dangerous to give a child an answer that you're not satisfied with yourself. Much better to say, "I don't know. What do you think?"

Nevertheless I responded: "Well, God did make everyone good, but every creature had to pass a test to see whether they would choose good for themselves. A lot of angels failed the test, and so did Adam and Eve."

Heather's face registered disgust at the weakness of this response.

"Well, I wouldn't have failed it," she stated resolutely. "If I'd had Eve's chance, without my genes being all messed up, you can bet your life I wouldn't have failed."

This conversation astonished me because I would never have dreamed of putting myself in Adam or Eve's place and thinking I could have done better. Is this because I've traveled too far from the garden-fresh innocence of childhood?

As I talked to Heather, it was almost as if she could remember being in Eve's shoes and seeing the possibility of a different choice and therefore of a radically different outcome to the entire course of human history. While I take sin for granted, Heather does not.

It's not that she's naive or unrealistic about sin. Around this same time she also told me, "I know that I could never, ever be good enough for God. I know I'm so bad that I don't deserve for Him to do one thing for me. I know He is so far above me that I could never do the least thing to make Him love me. But I also know He loves me anyway."

I doubt that I shall ever sum up the gospel better than this. Even so, as conscious as Heather is of being a sinner, she can still imagine herself back in Paradise and choosing not to sin.

The innocence of children is not innocence in the sense of being good through and through, as Jesus was. Rather it is the innocence of not comprehending evil. Children have no inkling of the enormity of wickedness, whereas adults know evil full well, which is why they pretend it is not as bad as all that.

The more I reflected on Heather's comment, the more I felt that she really wouldn't have done what Eve did, because sin is and always has been primarily an adult affair. Children sin because of adults. They sin because all the adults they know sin and because adults were sinning long before kids were even born.

This is why Heather can be righteously indignant over the atrocity of Eve, whereas I shrug it off as yesterday's news. Adults invented sin and bequeathed it to children. Eve, presumably, had to be a certain age before she could sin. She had to come of age, just as Jesus did, before Satan could properly test her.

Sin robs people of youth. The phrase "childlike sin" is an oxymoron. Goodness is childlike, but sin never is. Sin is cool, calculated, sophisticated, cynical. There is a sin called adultery, but there is no sin of "childery." Indeed children, like angels, possess a sexual neutrality, a freedom from sexual bondage that one does not sense in adults.

In the quote from Matthew at the head of this chapter, Jesus alluded to a direct link between children and angels and therefore between children and the throne of God. He might have put it this way: "Be careful how you treat children because they are closer to God than you are." This is like telling a drug pusher, "You'd better quit selling to kids because all the kids in this neighborhood are enrolled as undercover police agents."

Even secular society recognizes the relative innocence of children by exempting them from adult laws. The utter uniqueness of a child's perspective can be detected in Heather's innocent question, "Why didn't God make everyone good?" When adults ask this question, it usually indicates disgruntlement with God, but Heather was disgruntled with Eve—an entirely different matter. What a surprising twist!

Children are famous for asking, "Why?" They may be savages, but they are also little philosophers in their own right, and something about their why questions throws adults off guard. Faced with a "why," adults often give a rational explanation, when usually this is not what children want. Underneath every "why" lurks a more basic question. For example when Heather asks, "Dad, why do I have to go to school?" she may really be asking, "Why isn't there more love in the world?"

A child's "why" is different from ours; their "why" is really a "who." They want to know, "Who is looking after me?" and "Who can I trust?" A child's "why" can be like a Zen koan: Far from being meant to elicit a logical response, it's designed to break down logic. Adults do not like these kinds of questions. We live in an airtight world, and if we start playing with too many unanswerable questions, we become confused and depressed.

Adults like to have answers, but children like the questions. They especially like to stump adults. They can sense the world's noose being lowered over their heads, and they like anything that might stave off the hanging a little longer.

"Why's" are wise. Listen carefully to your children's questions and you may realize that they have just put their finger on some loophole in the adult view of reality. Through the loopholes, truth shines.

Like Adam and Eve, children live as if there is no one else in the whole world. In a sense, they're right. Every Christian likes to say, "Jesus died for me," but how many truly believe it? If I believe this, then I will also believe that God created the whole universe for me, that everything God has ever done was done just for me.

Isn't this preposterous? Not at all. God created the world for Adam—why wouldn't He do it for you? Granted, there are billions of others on this planet, but God still would have created the whole shebang just for you. Indeed—if you can grasp it—He did!

To believe this is not at all selfish. Narrow, yes—for "narrow [is] the road that leads to life" (Matthew 7:14). It is so narrow that you must walk it alone: you, with all your quirks, with all your unique and precious qualities. The gift of life was made to fit you like a glove. The world really is your oyster.

This perspective enables children to believe spontaneously in

God, which they all do until adults come along and show them how selfish they are. An innocent delight in oneself is part of the birthright of childhood that's bred out of us as we grow up.

I have an adult friend, Irene, who wakes up every morning and says, "Thank you so much, God, for the wonderful privilege of being Irene." She's thrilled by the idea that no one else in the world gets to be Irene. She knows that being Irene is an exquisitely precious gift reserved solely for her, and she aims to enjoy it to the full. I find it interesting that her very name means "peace." Irene is a woman at peace with herself because she loves being Irene.

How rare this is among adults! Yet all children, given half a chance, instinctively know they are precious and beautiful. Picture the tiny girl heading off to a birthday party dressed in a pretty pink frock. Look at her twirling in the center of the room, perfectly aware of all eyes upon her, yet also perfectly unselfconscious. Doesn't she know beyond a shadow of doubt that she's the prettiest, most adorable little thing in the world?

Her mother, meanwhile, dons a new dress and inspects herself critically in the mirror. Her daughter doesn't have to look in any mirror: She just knows she's beautiful!

The self-centeredness of children differs significantly from the self-centeredness of adults. Children plunge into life, whereas adults tend to guard and withhold themselves, never quite giving all. Children will give their all to the most ephemeral activities, squandering their best energies on trifles, whereas adults withhold themselves even from the most important things in life (including perhaps the most important of all: their kids).

Children are natural lovers of life, whereas adults are more like old married couples, disconnected from their first passion. Children, like puppies, are always ready at a moment's notice to bounce up and go exploring, adventuring, galivanting through the wide world. Adults, on the other hand, are always ready to sit a spell and rest their weary bones.

Children look at a crowded room, a packed schedule, an impossible situation, and their impulse is to add something to make it even more crowded, more packed, more impossible. (How well parents know this!) As a defense against the overwhelming bizarreness of life, children meet it head-on with something even more bizarre: themselves!

One sign of approaching adulthood is that the question "What am I going to do with my life?" moves increasingly to the fore. Adults are eager to distinguish themselves while children are content just to be themselves. Kids may fantasize about being ballerinas or firemen, but the issue holds no existential angst for them. Why should they worry about what they're going to be, when they already are? Ordinary existence seems very special to a child, fulfillment enough.

Of course, it is easy to idealize children. But Jesus was not concerned with this problem when He pointed to a child and said, "Be like this." He meant us to see that children really are freer, purer, more alive, that they are farther from death and have been more recently with God. As adults we cannot completely recapture the garden freshness of childhood, but by loving and admiring children we can breathe in their innocence like fresh air.

CHAPTER SEVEN

# THE STRONG-WILLED PARENT

*I tell you the truth, unless you change and become like little children,*
*you will never enter the kingdom of heaven.*

MATTHEW 18:3

This verse hit home to me one day in church when all the parents were encouraged to stand before their children and take their hands. As we looked into our children's eyes, the pastor read the above words.

Jesus first spoke these words in a similar setting. "He called a little child and had him stand among them" (v. 2). Jesus' point was that we, the adults, are the ones who must change. He illustrated this by having His disciples actually look at a child. "Whoever humbles himself like this child is the greatest in the kingdom of heaven" (v. 4).

This passage cannot be understood in the abstract, but only as you look into the eyes of a child you love and see that you must become like her, not try to make her like you.

For several years in a row we have attended a family camp run by a soft-hearted battle-ax of a woman named Thelma, who has tremendous authority and a skill for rubbing people's noses in plain common sense. The camp lasts seven days, the first five of which the children attend on their own. When the parents arrive on Friday night, Thelma sits us down and delivers an old-fashioned lecture about all the things we are doing wrong.

"All week long," she'll say, "we've had no problems with these children. They have been very good, very well-behaved. If you're having problems with your kids at home, I have to assume the problem is yours. So don't come running to me complaining about your kids, because I'll be on their side."

One father, after hearing this lecture for the third year, commented, "I think I've finally got the message. What she's saying is that the kids are fine. It's the parents who are screwed up."

People of my generation were fond of talking about the *strong-willed child*. If anybody was having trouble with their kids, it was because the kids were strong-willed. As young parents Karen and I were convinced we had a strong-willed child. There was no question about this. Any fool could see it. Heather's strong will was the source of all our problems with her.

As time went on, however, and I observed the parents of other strong-willed children, a simple realization began to dawn on me: Every so-called strong-willed child also had a strong-willed parent. Any fool could see this. So I began to wonder: Who's to blame?

Gradually I came to grasp two basic principles about strong wills:

First: They run in families. Symptoms such as obstinacy and

hyperactivity in children are both a sign and a direct result of the same traits in their parents.

Second: The way to treat a hyperactive child is for the parents to settle down, and the way to treat a strong-willed child is for the parents to soften their hearts.

In short, if you don't like your child's behavior, change your own. There are no bad children, there are only bad relationships.

A child is a stranger. Parents who have little love for their children feel this acutely. They feel no different than if some stranger off the street had moved in with them, or perhaps even an alien from another planet.

These parents never bargained on getting to know their child. They assume that because the child is of their own blood and has lived with them these many years, they must already know him or her. Certainly they know about as much as they care to. But really they do not know this person at all. Countless children grow up and move away from home without their parents ever getting to know them.

When it comes to children, to know is to like. If we do not love our children so much that we genuinely like them, with a strong, easygoing affection, we don't yet know who they are.

Until then, it is right that children should behave like strangers from another planet, for they really do come from somewhere else, and it takes them many years to learn the ropes of this alien world they have landed in. Children naturally do not like ropes. They do not understand the need for order, constraints, silence, indirection, or artificiality. All of this bewilders them. Imagine yourself plunked down into the streets of Bangkok or Beijing at rush hour, and you'll get a feel for how disorienting it can be to be a child among adults.

Although as adults we too know the feeling of being profoundly disoriented in our own familiar world, most of us are much better at suppressing this feeling. We've learned the ropes. But children know the world is not right and they cannot figure out why. They have come here from another place, and they cannot understand why things here are so messed up and why adults keep lying to them about it and denying that there is any real problem.

You do not think you are lying to your children? As parents we must understand that children do not listen to our words but to our actions. They have big ears but even bigger eyes. Though their hearing is selective, they see everything. Aren't we the same way with them? How often do we focus on a child's behavior yet fail to probe for or listen to the explanation behind it?

This means we must practice what we preach. The best teaching is by example, not precept. We do not even have the authority to teach any truth that is not deeply ingrained in our own lives. Hence James writes, "Not many of you should presume to be teachers, my brothers, because you know that we who teach will be judged more strictly" (3:1).

You parents—who disciplines you? Woe to those parents who administer harsher discipline to their children than they themselves are willing to accept from their heavenly Father! "First take the plank out of your own eye, and then you will see clearly to remove the speck from your brother's eye" (Matthew 7:5).

I am all in favor of giving children consequences for misbehavior. The problem comes when parents, forgetting that they too are but children, impose consequences they are not willing to accept for themselves.

For example, while Karen and I have always tried to insist that Heather be in bed on time, we ourselves chronically stay up too late and frequently struggle with a sleep deficit. I believe that because we have refused to change, we have never achieved much authority in this area with Heather.

The authority to discipline derives from a childlike acceptance of discipline for oneself. Jesus commended this in His encounter with the Roman centurion in Matthew 8. As the centurion put it, "I myself am a man under authority, with soldiers under me" (v. 9). Because he was used to both following and giving orders in a chain of command, this man believed that Jesus could issue orders in the spiritual realm and so heal his servant.

How interesting that the Roman commander described himself not as *having* authority but as being *under* authority. As a parent how would you describe your relation to authority? To exercise legitimate command you must be a person under command yourself, otherwise your authority will degenerate into authoritarianism.

I get nervous when parents quote from the book of Proverbs to back up their belief in corporal punishment. "He who spares the rod hates his son" (13:24) is a favorite, and "Folly is bound up in the heart of a child, but the rod of discipline will drive it far from him" (22:15).

What worries me is that Proverbs contains only a handful of such verses. Far more characteristic are sayings such as "Pleasant words promote instruction" (16:21), "Good understanding wins favor" (13:15), or "An offended brother is more unyielding than a fortified city" (18:19).

Do parents love to quote such verses? Not usually, because these maxims promote not the physical discipline of children but the spiritual discipline of adults.

The message of Proverbs is that a good and loving life, one full of the wisdom gleaned from childlike obedience to God, is the best discipline.

I remember Heather's first spanking. At about two years old, she threw a royal temper tantrum in the tub. Suddenly in anger I flipped her over and whacked her bottom.

I also recall the last spanking I gave her, when she was eight. This time I was so provoked that in the course of whacking her I sprained my knee and went around limping for days. No more spankings in our family.

On both occasions I disciplined in anger. Though even at the time I sensed this wasn't right, I reasoned: Doesn't my heavenly Father get angry with me? Sometimes it sure feels like it!

I know now that my real problem was not just anger but fear. "Never discipline in anger" is probably a good guideline, but a better one is "Don't discipline out of fear." Righteous anger is pure and clean because it is motivated by love. Unrighteous anger is motivated by fear.

If we're afraid of our children—of what they might do, or not do, or of all the ways they can hurt us—then our discipline will miss the mark because it does not arise from love. Indeed lack of love is the reason for our fear, for "there is no fear in love" (1 John 4:18). If we can get to the root of our fear, then appropriate discipline will follow naturally.

Ultimately good discipline arises neither from fear nor anger, but from sorrow. Wise discipline is not a reaction to misdeeds, but a sorrowful response to broken relationships.

As parents we should not focus upon the misdeed itself, but upon the threat misconduct poses to the quality of relationships. Paul touched on this issue when he wrote to the Corinthians, "We will be ready to punish every act of disobedience, once your obedience is complete" (2 Corinthians 10:6). With a child who constantly misbehaves and has a rebellious attitude, a great deal of misconduct must be overlooked. A parent must carefully pick and choose which acts to punish and let the rest go.

But with a good child—one whose basic attitude is loving compliance—even small acts of disobedience become highly significant. If a relationship with a child is already dysfunctional—why sweat? Mere discipline will never heal such a rift. But disruption in a good relationship can be mended by a word.

The chief qualification for good parenting is to have more love, more joy, and more peace than our children have. We need not be perfect, but we do need to be one step ahead.

The same principle holds true for all those in authority over others. A good pastor, for example, is not one who knows the Bible through and through and can preach up a storm. Rather, he is one who exhibits more of the fruit of the Spirit than his people and therefore can lead them into the light.

If as parents our lives are richer in freedom and in holy innocence than the lives of our children, we'll have little trouble guiding them. But pity the poor parents whose children are godlier than they!

It is impossible to lead people of any age who already know more than their leader. If our children are wiser than we are, we must admit our ignorance and become learners. Nothing is wiser than humility. When parents are humble enough to learn from their children, the children will accept this learning posture as wisdom.

This is childlikeness in action. Become a learner at your child's knee, and it will not be long before you pull ahead. After all, you are more experienced than they are in every way. All you lack is humility.

Golfers have a clear method of measuring their skill. They count their strokes and then compare that number with par. On the green it is a simple matter to determine whether they have sunk their putt or not.

Parenting is actually no more complicated than this. I can make it difficult for myself, but really as a parent I need only ask: Am I sinking my putts or not? Am I succeeding in connecting heart to heart with my child?

It's not such a stretch to compare children to holes on the golf course, for they too sit empty, expectant, waiting to be filled. Children will not move their position. No, parents must come to them. In their emptiness children are waiting to be filled with your love. You are the one with the big fancy bag of clubs. Do you know how to use them?

Strong-willed parents are like golfers who get angry at the little black hole for being too small, when really what is too small is the love in their hearts.

# PLAYFUL WORK, EARNEST PLAY

*I was the craftsman at his side.*
*I was filled with delight day after day,*
*rejoicing always in his presence.*

PROVERBS 8:30

The universe, to my eye, bears the marks of having been made by a child. It has the stamp of a child's mind, a child's hand, a child's rough-and-ready genius.

Look at a range of mountains silhouetted against the evening sky: Don't they resemble a child's paper cutouts? Or consider the duckbilled platypus, tigers and elephants, monkeypod trees and dandelions, mud and sand and snow, all those stars and planets and the vast emptiness of space: Could such things really be the products of an adult imagination?

Judgment, redemption, the church, the last days—these all bear signs of a mature, adult God at work. But creation itself—wild, magical, spontaneous, abstract, profligate—surely this was the act of a child at play.

Scripture tells us plainly that creation was indeed accomplished not by God the Father alone, but through His Son, who "was with God in the beginning. Through him all things were made; without him nothing was made that has been made" (John 1:2-3). Something about the Son's nature marked Him out for world making. In creation, as in the incarnation, while the Father supervised, the Son knelt in the muck of the world and got His hands dirty. After all, boys will be boys.

How many fathers would entrust such important work to their offspring? When I was young, my father sometimes asked me to join him while he did odd jobs around the house. My role, even as a teenager, was to stand by patiently and hand him tools, not to engage in the task itself. Really these were one-man jobs and I was to learn by watching, not by doing. When it came to cutting the grass or carrying out the garbage, this work I could do on my own. This was unskilled labor. But jobs requiring skill were for the father, not the son.

We glimpse quite a different picture in Proverbs 8, where the Son of God, speaking of His role in the creation of the world, describes Himself as "the craftsman at his side…filled with delight day after day" (v. 30). While the Father directed, the Son actually worked (or played with?) the raw materials of the new world, molding clay, sculpting rock, bending light in His fingers.

One Saturday when Heather was seven, I received a practical lesson in how a complex task could be accomplished not just with my child, but through her. The task was the assembling of a car-top carrier. Since we were due to leave on a road trip the next day, the job had to be done quickly and well. Karen had gone for the afternoon, leaving me alone with Heather. At seven she was not old enough to operate a screwdriver or a wrench, right? At least, not old enough to feed a myriad of bolts and washers correctly into their housings and tighten them securely. Right?

Wrong. For the first hour we had a thoroughly frustrating time of it. Dad was not amused about having a little craftsman at his side. Far from being filled with delight, Heather was soon filled with rage. Finally, not because I believed she could do it but only to get her off my back, I let her have a wrench and a few bolts. She could horse around, I'd keep a sharp eye out, and after she went to bed I'd redo her part.

This was a nice plan, but I had only one set of tools. Every time I reached for a tool, it was exactly the one Heather wanted. Of course all along I'd been in no mood for a cooperative venture. This was a one-man job.

Heather quickly took over as the one man. At first the sheer force of her determination shouldered me aside. Gradually another factor emerged: skill. With growing amazement I realized that Heather was doing a perfectly fine job. In the end she completed the lion's share of the work all by herself, with nothing but her two pudgy hands and a few words of direction from me. I functioned as little more than a glorified supervisor.

And guess what? I loved it. I loved it because, in a way too profound for my conventional adult mind to have envisioned, we two, father and daughter, were truly working together. I loved it because I was bursting with pride in my little girl. I loved it because a job I had pictured as tedious was transformed into a source of delight and astonishment.

Is this what God the Father feels like? A Glorified Supervisor of the universe rejoicing in the accomplishments of His kids?

The revelation of God as a Trinity invites parents and children to work together in a common spirit. But how often does this happen?

When Heather was twelve she had the ceiling of her room painted dark blue because she wanted to decorate it with glow-in-the-dark stars. Having obtained a ceiling-sized stencil of stars in the summer sky, she and I put on some music and spent an afternoon dabbing thick blobs of fluorescent paint into hundreds of holes of varying sizes. After three hours of this, our necks were reminding us of Michelangelo's work on the Sistine ceiling. Heather even commented that she had a new appreciation for what Jesus (to accomplish another kind of work) must have gone through hanging on the cross.

Toward the end of this project, we faced the task of creating the Milky Way. This required cutting a broad swatch out of the stencil and using a toothbrush to spray on thousands of tiny dots to give the effect of clouds of stars. Worried about paint spillage, I suggested that I should do this part by myself.

"No way!" Heather objected.

"But I could be more careful than you."

"Dad, don't be silly. The universe isn't careful. There are stars exploding out there!"

So Heather did the toothbrush spraying. The only paint spilled was in the bathroom where to this day it creates an interesting effect.

Adults largely avoid working with children because children have an unnerving habit of turning work into play. This drives adults crazy because we tend to be so goal-oriented. Adults know too well what children have yet to learn: Work is supposed to be drudgery. Children are not yet enslaved by work, nor do they intend to be. They are quite content living all day long in a big, happy playground.

When it comes to work, children must eventually learn that being responsible, serving others, and doing honest labor can be good for the soul. Adults must learn that the soul of all work is play.

Do you play? Do you play with your kids? Even more important: Do you spend time, as children do, playing by yourself? If you never play alone, you'll probably never play—really play—with anyone else.

Children don't play because they are four years old; they play because they are free of worries and a world of wonder lies before them begging to be explored. A child's life is not a bed of roses. Their lot can be just as difficult as ours, yet in the midst of the darkest, most twisted circumstances, something in a child keeps reaching for, and finding, the light.

I've heard people tell of infants grasping at sunbeams. When

Heather was about eighteen months old, she ran down the street toward the rising full moon, shouting, "Catch it! Catch it!" She was in earnest. I don't think she'd ever noticed the moon before. She was learning to catch balls, and she really thought she could reach out and catch the moon too.

All of us are children at heart, but we need children to remind us of this. Children are a bridge to our more innocent past. In German the word for child is *kind*, which gives us our word *kindergarten*. Related to this is the word *kindling*, meaning little sticks that set big ones on fire. Why not get close to children and let them kindle your heart? Reach for the moon and the stars and set your world on fire!

Being with children enlivens and humbles us in a way that time spent with adults cannot. It is wonderful when adults play together, but it is never quite the same as playing with children who, after all, invented play. Children hold the original patent on play, imagination, naiveté, exploration. We need to go to the source to have these fires rekindled.

One spring morning when Heather was heading out to the barn for her riding lesson, she called to me to bring her a couple of carrots for her horse. I'd slept badly and was feeling grumpy, but as I took the carrots down to Heather in the garage, an impulse seized me. Handing one carrot to Heather and keeping the other myself, I pointed mine straight at her and announced, "En garde!"

For the next five minutes we engaged in a furious duel of clashing carrots, chasing each other all around the car while thrusting and parrying, dodging and squealing and hooting. When finally we called a truce and stood there winded, all at once I found myself nearly collapsing on the floor in a rollicking, unstoppable belly laugh.

Who would have guessed that a grumpy, unbreakfasted, middle-aged man could have so much laughter in him? Needless to say, that laugh transformed my day. I just couldn't get over the utter absurdity of it: me, Mike Mason, mild-mannered, respectable adult, dueling with carrots in his garage!

On a nostalgic trip to my hometown I happened to meet some people from the neighborhood where I'd grown up. I asked them if they remembered an old playmate of mine named Donald Frost.

"Don Frost!" they exclaimed. "Sure we know him. Haven't you heard—he's a well-known sculptor now. His parents still live on this street, and his studio's not far from here."

I couldn't have been more surprised. Having left this neighborhood at four, I had few memories, but I vividly recalled Don Frost because I'd once pushed him off a concrete embankment into a tub of water and was soundly spanked for it. Could it be true that this little fellow really had grown up to make a big splash in the world?

If Don Frost had become a financial planner, I probably would have left it at that. But the thought that a friend from my earliest childhood days had developed into a professional artist, a man after my own heart—this piqued my curiosity. I had to look him up.

So the next day I found myself in Don Frost's studio, watching him demonstrate how two liquid chemicals mixed together would puff up to thirty times their volume and harden into a wonderful sculpting material. Then he took some vials of paint additive and brushed sample streaks onto a board. Eyes popping, his whole face aglow with excitement, he cried, "Look at the intensity of these colors!" He could have been a kid playing with his first chemistry set.

Then he showed me his portfolio. He has two quite distinct styles, one figurative, the other abstract. He told me that the figures (mainly human) sell the best, but that the abstracts are what he loves doing.

Though I liked all his work, the abstracts appealed to me most. Graceful, dancelike, musical, they resemble the shapes oil might make while falling through water if you could freeze its sinuous whorls.

"What's in your mind as you're creating one of these?" I asked him.

"Oh, nothing at all!" Don laughed. "I'm just playing. I'll be fiddling around with Plasticine, and I'll see a line or a shape I like, and I'll think, 'That's beautiful!' And I'll want to sculpt it."

The words "I'm just playing" burned themselves into my memory. Imagine—after all these years my little friend Donald Frost is *still playing!* This visit occurred just a few weeks before I sat down to write *The Mystery of Children.* It was important to be reminded that the mainspring of all art—indeed of life itself—is pure play.

Each one of us has an artist inside. And what is an artist but a child who has never lost the gift of looking at life with curiosity and wonder? In *Peter Pan* J. M. Barrie wrote about the Neverland that "on these magic shores children at play are for ever beaching their coracles. We too have been there; we can still hear the sound of the surf, though we shall land no more."[4]

I wonder. It seems to me that if we do not land regularly in the country of childhood, we'll turn out as pretty dried-up, stodgy adults. Children are living proof that it is actually possible to take Jesus' advice, "Do not worry about tomorrow, for tomorrow will worry about itself" (Matthew 6:34). Adults, of course, expend much energy discounting this proof. We love to make excuses for why our lives are so hamstrung and fettered. "I have duties and responsibilities," we say. "I have housework and a job to do, finances to watch, appointments to keep. Besides, I've got all these kids to look after!"

All this is true. Adults do bear greater responsibility, but is this an excuse to live without joy and spontaneity? Is this a good reason to be bitter and careworn, our souls pinched with ingratitude as we walk around looking like death warmed over?

NOOOOOOOOOOOOOOO!!! This is the great lie we bought from Satan when we left childhood behind. This is why Peter Pan never wanted to grow up. He saw the worries, the wrinkles, the grinding responsibility, the haunting march of death, and he wasn't having it. He dug in his heels and refused to budge.

Naturally, he missed a lot. In Neverland he never fell in love, never married, never had kids of his own, and so on. Poor, pagan waif. No one ever told him about Jesus Christ who promised that anyone who believes in Him will "live forever" and "will never see death" (John 6:51; 8:51). According to Jesus, there is a way to grow up without taking on all the grim baggage of adulthood, a way to remain always like a child.

Steven Spielberg's movie *Hook* is the story of a grown man named Peter who finds his way back to the Neverland. It's an arduous, nearly impossible journey, but he undertakes it because his children are slipping away from him and he's desperate to win them back.

In the film Captain Hook kidnaps the children. This symbolizes the fact that Peter has completely lost touch with his children and indeed with the child inside himself. To reconnect, he must revert to childhood and learn again how to play.

When Peter finally does burst through the barrier to reenter his childhood, naturally he wants to stay there and keep on playing forever. Yet he knows he cannot. He is not a child merely, but an adult too. He is not one or the other but both.

As an adult he has certain responsibilities, but as a child he has certain freedoms. To fulfill his role as a father, he must draw fully upon both sides of his nature. He cannot pretend that he can play all the time and never grow up, yet neither can he neglect play and never stoop to the level of his children. To save his children, he must become a child himself and then fight for them as only an adult can.

Isn't this what our heavenly Father did for us through Jesus Christ? He became a little child who before our eyes grew up into a man and saved us.

# CHAPTER EIGHT

# THE CHILD JESUS

*People were bringing little children to Jesus*
*to have him touch them....*
*And he took the children in his arms,*
*put his hands on them and blessed them.*

MARK 10:13,16

Do you ever ponder what Jesus was like as a boy? At Christmas we
have all stood with the shepherds and peered down with wonder at
the swaddled incarnation in the manger. We know the Baby Jesus.

But do we know the Child Jesus? Do we know the quiet, con-
tented, playful little boy, happy as the day is long and completely
untroubled by the world's ills? Do we know the wrestling, tickling,
howling-with-glee Jesus? Do we know the laughing One who runs
through the fields with the wind in His hair? Do we know the
Cool Dude Jesus, the outrageously alive, devil-may-care teenager,
swaggering, sauntering, skateboarding through the streets of our
town as if He owned them?

At different times in my Christian journey, I find myself praying to the Father, to the Son, to the Holy Spirit, or to all three.

Each member of the Trinity has a distinct personality, and the help of each one seems appropriate for different circumstances.

In the same way, at various times I find myself relating to different aspects of Jesus or to different phases in His life. Sometimes it is the babe in the manger whom I love, or the young adult struggling with the awareness of His identity, or the grown man at the height of His ministry. Other times I worship the risen Lord, or the glorious returning King, or the Lamb with "seven horns and seven eyes" (Revelation 5:6).

Yet Jesus was also a child, and the Child Jesus inspired the writing of this book. Devotion to the Divine Child refreshes my stale theology, challenges my rationalism, shocks and outrages me, and renews my springs of wonder and spontaneous play.

The fact that God entrusted Himself to us in this way, that He opened His arms and embraced the world as a child, living His obscure and ordinary life as a small boy just like me—somehow this speaks to me as loudly as the cross.

When Jesus opened the eyes of a man born blind, He asked him, "Do you believe in the Son of Man?" (John 9:35). The question was not, "Do you believe in the Christ?" No, Jesus' choice of words implied more than this.

Jesus' question was tantamount to saying, "Do you believe in the Christ Child? Do you believe that the Messiah will come as a child? Do you believe that in the fullness of time the human race itself will become, as it were, pregnant by the Holy Spirit and will give birth to a child who will be a new kind of being, one entirely without sin, who will in turn impart His radical, new form of life to everyone who believes in Him?"

A stirring thought! Do you believe it? Do you believe that the whole world, led by a divine child, can be made young again?

To know Jesus is to know the heart of a child. Even after Jesus grew up, He remained a child of God. Being a Son was the essence of His identity, the way He chiefly saw Himself. He continually referred to Himself as "Son": either the "Son of God," the "Son of Man," or simply "the Son." He was always somebody's boy.

A child is not something one can be independently. Being a child implies having a parent. A child *belongs* to somebody. The word *adult* is self-referencing but the word *child* clearly denotes both lineage and dependency. An adult stands alone but a child is *somebody's*.

While Jesus knew He was the Christ, the Messiah, the Savior of the world, such titles meant little to Him. He did not define Himself by titles but by a relationship. Principally He was a child, a son, *the* Son of His Father.

Jesus saw everyone else this way too. He saw people as children, the children of God. He referred to His disciples as "my children" (John 13:33). Can you imagine yourself at thirty-three speaking this way to a group of full-grown men, some of them your seniors? Coming from Jesus this was not the least patronizing, for He knew He was but a child Himself.

God not only sees us all as children and exhorts us to be

childlike, He also showed us the way by being a perfect child Himself. Jesus was the model child, the paragon of loving obedience. He loved His Father passionately and purely and did everything according to His Father's will. We can never truly understand Jesus until we see that He did nothing on His own, but thought and spoke and acted only out of love for His Father.

He said, "I have come down from heaven not to do my will but to do the will of him who sent me" (John 6:38). Again: "I tell you the truth, the Son can do nothing by himself; he can do only what he sees his Father doing, because whatever the Father does the Son also does" (John 5:19).

Do you see how Jesus' whole life showed the beauty and power of perfect filial love? If only we could catch a glimpse of this love and feel the motivating force of it! Then, instead of exhausting ourselves by burning independent energy, we could say contentedly as Jesus did, "I do nothing on my own" (John 8:28).

Imagine having a son like Jesus, a son who obeyed your every wish, who fulfilled your wildest dreams, who somehow completed you by doing work that was beyond your reach. Then imagine this son saying about every one of his accomplishments, "I owe it all to my Dad. He's the one to thank. It's really all his doing. I couldn't do anything without him."

Sound far-fetched? Yes, it's not a common picture, but this is how things work in the heavenly family, and this is the pattern to which all earthly families must conform more and more. God's love is great and the love of Jesus is great. But the greatest love is that *between* the Father and the Son through the Holy Spirit. To be caught up in this love is to know God as He is: not a bachelor but a family.

Paul begins a well-known prayer, "I kneel before the Father, from whom his whole family in heaven and on earth derives its name" (Ephesians 3:14-15). I never understood this verse until I learned that in Greek the word for father, *pater,* has the same root as the word for family, *patria.* (A *patria* may also be a family of families, that is, a nation or fatherland.)

Even in English the words for *father* and *family* are intimately connected. This is exactly Paul's point: Everything to do with families derives directly from God, the Father of all. Obviously the physical capacity to produce children derives from God. Isn't it also obvious that the capacity to be good parents comes from Him? Who of you by thinking can put together bones and flesh to create a child? Similarly, good parenting does not come from thinking, taking courses, or reading books, but from our heavenly Father.

We cannot be part of a family by our own efforts. A family has to do with who we are, not what we do. Some people chafe against life on the grounds that they never chose to be born in the first place. Of course not! Life is not a matter of human will but of birth. Entering the family of God and being His child is not an accomplishment but a realization.

I find it remarkable that Jesus, although perfect and sinless, wasn't that different from everyone else. Different, yes—but how amazingly assimilated He was! He lived in the world for over thirty years before anyone (except maybe His parents) caught on to who He was. Even at the height of His popularity not many recognized Him as God. To most people He was just Jesus of Nazareth, the carpenter's son, possibly a prophet.

Sanctity may be a more ordinary thing than we thought. Could it be that goodness, saintliness and love are all less obviously resplendent than we imagine? If so, this is good news, for the less exalted such qualities appear, the more accessible they become. Jesus preached, "The kingdom of God is near" (Mark 1:15). Maybe it's closer than we think?

In the Campus Crusade film known simply as *Jesus*, my favorite scene lasts five seconds. You may have watched this film many times and never noticed this particular scene. It occurs early in the film, just after Jesus has spent forty days fasting in the wilderness and being tempted by Satan. It shows Jesus' first act as He returns to civilization full of the Holy Spirit. What will He do with so much power? Perform some great miracle? Deliver a profound sermon? Take hold of a thunderbolt and strike the earth?

Watch:

Jesus enters a busy market square in a village. He sees a young girl. He smiles at her, a smile of radiant warmth, and says one word: "Hello."

The girl smiles back, beautifully, and answers, "Hello."

That is all. Nothing else happens. Five seconds.

Scripture does not record this incident, but I believe everything Jesus is can be summed up by a simple smile and hello exchanged with a child. Surely this smile is what the forty-day fight with Satan in the desert was all about. And this is why the fight had to be carried on to the cross. Jesus came to earth to bring the smile of God's love to the faces of His children, and at all costs the devil sought to stop this divine smile from dawning upon the rough old world.

Most people find it difficult to grasp how free, natural and happy is the love of Jesus. If only the world had reacted like the child in the film, instantly lighting up in recognition of God's smile! And if only the church today were a childlike, smiling church, quick to see our Lord in one another!

My friend Adam West has a motto: "Never let a day go by without bringing a smile to the face of a child." Before he was married, Adam traveled a lot. Eating frequently in restaurants, he enjoyed watching families with small children. Usually the adults in these groups had a painfully obvious agenda: Stuff the kids with food and do the bare minimum to keep them busy so that mom and dad could grab a few moments of peace and maybe even enjoy a grown-up conversation.

Adam knew that what mom and dad wanted to talk about was not interesting. He was more interested in the kids. He liked trying to get their attention. From a nearby table he'd make eyes at them, pull faces, stick his fingers in his ears, cock his head sideways, and raise his eyebrows. Stuff like that.

If Adam could get a kid to notice him, that was a first-base hit.

If the kid stared at him with wide-eyed wonder, that was a double.

A smile or a laugh scored a triple-bagger.

And if Adam could get a kid out of his seat and walking toward him across a crowded restaurant, that was a home run and Adam's day was made.

The modern world is like a packed, noisy McDonald's restaurant. Imagine yourself sitting in one of its stiff, uncomfortable chairs and eating its unnourishing food. Like a child whose parents are preoccupied, you feel vaguely lonely, bored, edgy.

Looking across the room, all at once you see a funny man. His head is cocked sideways and he's making faces at you. You realize he's trying to get your attention.

Amused, flattered, warmed inside, you ease out of your chair and start making your way across the room. As you draw closer to the man, he drops his bizarre antics, straightens up and flashes a radiant smile. It's as if he is greeting an old friend. You feel you have never seen such a beautiful, welcoming smile, a smile that touches and warms the deepest place in you. Smiling back, you know that never before in your life have you felt so good, so happy, so natural, so yourself. You've found an instant friend.

You go up to the man and introduce yourself, and he tells you his name.

"Hello," he says. "My name is Jesus."

# A CHRISTMAS STORY

*From the lips of children and infants*
*you have ordained praise*
*because of your enemies,*
*to silence the foe and the avenger.*

PSALM 8:2

Christmas morning, 1995.

We're sitting in the living room around the tree. We've barely begun to open presents, but already eight-year-old Heather is dragging out the one from Daddy, crying, "I want this one."

"No, Heather," I say for about the tenth time. "That's a special one, and I'd like you to save it till last."

"But I want it NOWWWWWW!" she wails.

Already she's grabbing at the ribbon. What to do? Snatch the box away? In my mind I picture a vicious physical struggle over a Christmas present, a little girl hot with tears bolting furiously from the room, Karen glaring at me reproachfully, Christmas Day in ruins.

At the same time, I'm thinking about the contents of this box. It's important to me that this special gift be left until the end. It's especially important that Heather not open it in her present state: grasping, whining, impudent. Spoiled rotten.

"Heather, please don't open that now. I beg you."

"Daddy, don't be silly. It's my present. I can open it if I want."

She tears the paper.

"Heather—Stop! Please!"

But it's too late. The bare box is exposed and now the lid is coming off. Now the tissue paper is parting...

Okay, okay, I tell myself. Lean back, take a deep breath. Get a grip. The special present is ruined, but it's not the end of the world.

And then, all at once—a miracle! Who would have dreamed that such a thing could happen?

Heather is crying! Sobbing. As the contents of the box are laid bare, she sobs and sobs as if her heart would burst.

Karen and I lean closer, put our arms around her. All together we gaze at the object in the box, as still the crying goes on and on...

Now let me back up to the night before, Christmas Eve. It's getting on to midnight, and after a busy week I'm aching for bed. But there's one more job I must do, a job that was supposed to be easy but, like most manual tasks I undertake, it's developed a bizarre complication.

I'm seated in a halo of light at my grandfather's old oak desk. In one hand I hold a wooden cross about eighteen inches long, and in the other a plastic figure of Jesus in a loincloth with His arms out-stretched. I'm trying to fit the two together.

On the desk sits a tube of contact cement, beside it a small bottle of epoxy. Both substances have utterly failed to accomplish their intended purpose. I'm about to go down to the basement to fetch the hot glue gun, but I can tell you right now, that isn't going to work either.

The problem is that Jesus is warped. His hands and His feet are not on a level plane, so that every time I try to stick Him down, He pops up again. This plastic is really springy stuff.

Finally I grow so exasperated that I'm about ready to use nails. At that point, I turn the whole mess over to Karen, who of course with her womanly arts accomplishes it easily.

And so to bed.

Only once before in her life have I heard Heather cry the way she cried that Christmas morning. The other time, we were in church singing worship songs. At least, Karen and I were singing. At that age Heather was more likely to be reading, drawing, fidgeting, talk-ing, or rummaging around for food.

All at once, for no apparent reason, she burst into tears. Differ-ent kinds of crying have different sounds, and instantly I knew that this was no ordinary crying over a pinched finger or a thwarted desire. This was weeping.

Have you ever heard a child weep? The crying of angels, I

suppose, could hardly have a sound more surprising, more holy, more heartrendingly pure.

Heather wept for a long, long time, and when she finally ceased, our little girl's face looked like a freshly bloomed rose washed in dew in the first light of morning.

Later when we asked her what had happened, she said simply, "I saw an angel light." Back then I was working on a book about angels, and I'd mentioned to her that some people see angels not in the form of figures, but as colored lights.

Glancing up toward the church balcony that morning, Heather had seen a circular light composed of many beautiful colors. This is what had touched her heart, and for long afterward she referred to this experience as her "vision."

Now it's Christmas morning, and once again I'm hearing the sound of my daughter weeping. Only this time it's not a vision she's seeing, it's something solid and tangible. An object.

The object Heather is crying over is a crucifix. Jesus on the cross.

Her crying is deep, savage, tender, wrenchingly repentant.

She had wanted a crucifix. Asked for it. I have one in my study that I received as a gift at the age of fourteen on the occasion of my confirmation in the Anglican Church. I did not become a Christian until many years later, in the meantime sowing a lot of wild oats. But for some reason, wherever I went, I kept that crucifix hanging on my wall.

Heather, looking at it one day, asked if she could have one for her room. I was pleased. Overjoyed, in fact. I'd far rather give her Jesus than Barbie.

So off I went to the Catholic bookstore (really more of a jewelry or hardware store) to look at crucifixes. I couldn't find one that I liked. It was two days before Christmas, hardly the right season. Maybe their Easter stock was low.

In the end I had to buy the cross and the figure separately, and that is why I spent Christmas Eve trying to affix Jesus to His cross and finding out that He didn't want to go.

The next day I could hardly wait for Heather to open her special present. But it had to be last, after the orgy of materialism. That way we could move easily into a time of family devotions. Every year this is a challenge, trying to slip the Bible in among the presents without Heather's noticing.

This year, instead of the Christmas story from Luke, I planned to read the story of Good Friday and Easter. It would be a different sort of Christmas, a memorable one.

Yet never in my fondest imaginings could I have predicted just how different and memorable this Christmas would be.

Heather's weeping went on and on…and on and on…

The three of us sat there huddled on the couch until, finally, the sobbing subsided. Heather still hadn't taken the crucifix out of its box. Now she began to touch it, delicately, exploratively, until eventually lifting it in her hands.

By this point the room was filling up with a kind of warm, rich, golden glow. All of us felt it. We were all teary, tenderized, bright-eyed, touched to the core. It was as if God Himself had opened us up like Christmas gifts, exposing our soft and real hearts and touching them with His fingers.

What happened then was no canned devotional time, but the most beautiful and spontaneous worship I have ever experienced. With God right there in the room, what else could we do but thank and praise Him and lift our voices in hymns and carols? We even got up and danced around the Christmas tree for pure joy.

Oh yes—Jesus would not stay on His cross that day! He would not be glued down and hung on a wall! For close to an hour an eight-year-old girl completely forgot all the rest of her presents, still waiting to be opened, and celebrated one present only, the one gift that she suddenly knew to be better than all other gifts in the world put together.

What came out of the box that Christmas morning was no mere crucifix, but Jesus Himself—Jesus alive, royally well, and bursting with happiness. More than a gift, this was the Giver Himself.

# CHAPTER NINE

# THE CHILD WITHIN

*You created my inmost being;*
*you knit me together in my mother's womb.*
*I praise you because I am fearfully and wonderfully made.*

PSALM 139:13-14

About a month before I became a Christian, toward dawn on August 11 of my thirtieth year (I recall the date precisely because I'd stayed up late to watch the annual Perseid meteor shower), I had a vivid hypnopompic vision. I saw myself just as if I were outside myself and observing me across a room. As I began walking toward myself, I felt the two of us were going to merge into one. What a glorious sensation that would be—to step right into myself!

But instead, as I drew close to my double, the other me began to grow younger, in a rapid succession of stages, until eventually I was standing before myself just as I had been at the age of six. Seeing myself so cute and innocent, with all the charming attractiveness of youth, I experienced an enormous nostalgia for my lost childhood and an overwhelming desire to kiss and embrace myself.

But at this point—alas!—the little boy turned away from me,

obviously repulsed. He wanted nothing to do with me. Knowing that I was loathsome to myself, I wept bitterly.

When Jesus exhorted us to "receive the kingdom of God like a little child" (Luke 18:17), He was not thinking of just any child. He was thinking of a particular child: the one who lives inside of you.

No one can be a good parent without first being a good child. A father can get down on the floor and play with his toddler, but if he never gets down on the floor of his own heart to connect with the little boy in himself, he'll never be free. If he never remembers what it was like when his Dad yelled at him, then he'll keep on yelling at his own kids. If he never feels pity and tenderness for the child he once was, he'll never feel pity or tenderness at all. If he never feels his own littleness, he'll walk around forever carrying a big stick. If he never enters the secret, intimate place of his own childhood, he'll never find intimacy with anyone else.

The term *inner child* has long been a catch phrase in popular psychology. But what does it mean? I believe the inner child is our spirit. Looking at a child is as close as we can come to seeing the spirit or inner essence of a human being.

Jesus wants us to become like children because our spirits lived closest to the surface during childhood. In childhood our hearts were the most transparent, most vulnerable, most malleable. Growing up usually means covering up our spirit more and more with flesh. God wants us to become the person we really are inside, the person we were born to be. Becoming childlike involves peeling away the masks to get back to the real, rosy-cheeked, bright-eyed face beneath.

Once a child, always a child. If you were ever three years old, a part of you will always be three. Though I am now forty-eight, I am also thirty-eight, twenty-eight, eighteen and eight. All these ages are wrapped up in me. I have lived them day by day and they are mine.

At times I'll find the eight-year-old in me peeking around the corner, or the three-year-old sneaking up on me like a remembered smell. An odd experience, a crisis, a twinge of nostalgia can catapult me back into the feeling of a previous age. A clerk in a store gives me a strange look, and all at once I am six again, and the proof is the sudden frustration, the twinge of fear, or perhaps even the joy that seems to well up out of nowhere.

When my friend Chris had a new baby daughter, he marveled at the way everyone who saw Danica was transformed by her presence. Gruff, noisy, hairy adults would grow suddenly soft-hearted, a new gentleness enveloping them, an otherworldly light suffusing their features as they peered down at the little fist of a face nestled in the blankets.

What was it, Chris wondered, that people saw in Danica? Almost as soon as he asked this question, the answer came: They saw the image of God. What else could elicit such a remarkable transformation? Seeing the divine spark so freshly kindled in an infant reminded people of the essential wonder and glory of being human.

"Why does it take a baby to bring this out in us?" Chris reflected. "Shouldn't we all be seeing the image of God in each other? Aren't we surrounded by images of God that are forty years old, or sixty, or eighty?"

To see the image of God, we must see the child in one another. No adult relationship can thrive until we see the other's child and relate also to that little one.

Imagine you are sitting in your boss's office as he chews you out over some costly mistake in business. Now imagine that your boss suddenly transforms before your eyes into the mewling little baby he once was. Or try imagining him at fourteen months taking his first steps, or throwing his pudgy arms around the knees of a giantess and crying, "Mommy, I love you!"

Doesn't this change the way you feel about your boss?

Try looking this way at the famous and the powerful. This sex starlet, for example, was once just a little ball of pudge, and the military dictator began life exactly as we all did, a babe in arms. Seeing the infants, the tots, the toddlers that adults once were rejuvenates old habits of relating. Wouldn't it be fun to see everyone this way, reduced to adorable vulnerability? Wouldn't you love them more?

Consider the effect of looking this way at Christ, as we do each year at Christmas. Perhaps the best way to know Jesus is to see Him through the eyes of His own mother, the one who nursed Him at her breast, who saw His first smile, heard His first word, and who "treasured up all these things and pondered them in her heart" (Luke 2:19).

What if you could see yourself this way? What if you could catch a glimpse of your own spirit? What if you could step out into your backyard right now and see yourself at three years old playing on the grass?

How compelling, satisfying, and strangely powerful is the image of the child! Paradoxically, there's a wholeness about children that makes every other stage of life seem oddly incomplete. Put an adult and a child side by side, and the adult looks washed out, pale, not quite so alive. Not older merely, but nearer death. Though the adult is taller, the candle of life has burnt lower.

Now look at the child: angelic, fair, eyes twinkling, hair shining, the wax of the skin still fresh and smooth. In the smaller package there's a sense of contained energy. The mystery is greater. So much to do and to be, so much life to live. Truly, said Jesus, "The kingdom of heaven belongs to such as these" (Matthew 19:14).

I enjoy talking to people about their childhoods. I like to ask questions such as:

"What were you like as a little girl?"

"What was your main characteristic as a child?"

"When you were little what did you need that you never got?"

When these questions are asked in an appropriate setting, it is surprising how often people's eyes will moisten. Even a strong, normally unemotional man may grow teary. Some people will break down and sob. Others may cry a bit and then suddenly pull themselves together and become quite guarded, defensive, even angry.

I have observed these reactions many times. It's clear to me that people go through much of their lives never once giving a thought to the tender little child they once were. To have someone call up this memory is like taking the cap off a deep well. One brief smell of the sweet, pure water of childhood drives people so mad with intoxicated longing that they must immediately stuff the cap back on the well. They cannot allow the little child within to be real, let alone believe it is possible to make actual contact with her.

What they do believe, you see, is that their little child is dead. She died a long time ago. This is where the tears come from, tears of unresolved grief.

According to George Lucas, the central question in his *Star Wars* films is "How do we get Darth Vader back? How do we get him back to that little boy that he was in the first movie, that good person who loved and was generous and kind? Who had a good heart?"[5]

I believe the way to recover the lost inner child is to follow deep emotion, the feelings of the heart. For that is what a child is: a bundle of pure feelings, raw sensation. Children think, but their thinking is not like ours, not rational. This is why explanations never satisfy them. One needs rational ability to accept the contradictions inherent in explanations. Emotion cannot accept a compromise.

Children do not have what adults call a "mind-set." Their world-view is not set but is continually in flux. In a single day they will see the world in a dozen different ways. They are explorers, experimenters, entrepreneurs of the heart.

We cannot encounter the child within us except by reentering this formative flux. We must unhinge our mind-set and return the mind to a state of radical development. We need to stop thinking so much and allow ourselves to feel. Taking it for granted that we do not know ourselves well, we must seek self-knowledge in subtle stirrings, ambushes of emotion, odd moments of recognition.

For example, in the midst of pursuing some well-intentioned goal, I might notice that instead of having a good time I'm feeling nervous, frightened, or bored. Conversely, in some apparently humdrum situation I might suddenly feel an upsurge of joy or excitement, or perhaps just a quiet peace.

Where do these feelings come from? What are they about? Often this is not immediately clear. But if sitting on a church committee makes me feel insecure and angry, then I'll stop doing it. And if sitting still for an hour and looking out the window brings me peace and a mysterious sense of fulfillment, then I'll do more of that.

This method of living from the heart sounds so simple and straightforward. Yet hardly anyone follows it. Instead people seem committed to their own unhappiness. Very few have the courage to follow spontaneous heartfelt promptings in naive simplicity as children do.

After years of witnessing my daughter's freewheeling lifestyle, I had to admit I was jealous. Jealous of her spontaneous engagement with life, while like a Pharisee I remained stuck in the mud of sullen disconnectedness. Time to do some catching up. If I wanted to be closer to my daughter, I had to get inside the skin of the little boy within me.

One morning I was praying when, unbidden, images from my early childhood rose before me, accompanied by tears. Though at the time I did not understand what was happening, I knew that what lay behind those tears must be vastly important. On the strength of this experience, I embarked on a conscious pilgrimage to rediscover my lost childhood.

While some people have vivid memories of their childhood, I had few. My childhood seemed like a locked room that I could not enter. But when a chance arose to see the house where I had spent the first four years of my life, on impulse I thought, *Why shouldn't I enter?*

A house where you have lived is always your house. Titles and deeds are mere pieces of paper compared to the more substantial claims of memories that, ghostly yet nonetheless real, cling to hallways, staircases, corners, windows, closets. Walls never forget. They've heard your laughter and your tears, been smeared by your own stubby, grubby fingers, echoed to the pounding of your tiny excited feet. You yourself have forever hallowed these places by your presence.

How surprised I was to discover that the people who now owned my house were the same ones who had bought it from my family over forty years ago. As it happened, they had returned home from an errand just moments before I knocked on their door and introduced myself. They happily invited me in.

Thanks to their hospitality, I was able to see the window in my bedroom where the tree branches used to scrape against the glass as I tried to fall asleep.

*Is this why I'm still such a light sleeper?*

I saw the triangular crawlspace where my sister and I played at dress-up.

*Is this why I feel so safe in small, dark rooms?*

I saw the bathroom where I fell and put my teeth through my tongue, leaving a deep gash that remains to this day.

*Is this why I shrink from public speaking?*

Best of all was the driveway. My favorite picture of myself as a little boy shows me standing in this driveway on a winter day, cocooned in a snowsuit and staunchly holding up one black-mittened hand straight in front of me as if to halt a speeding locomotive. The look on my face says plainly, "Stop right there! One more inch and you'll have *me* to deal with!"

Forty-five years later I stood on this same spot, assumed this same grim pose, and had my picture taken with tears streaming down my face.

Today these two photos sit side by side on my desk. After so many years of letting life's locomotives run me over, it's hard sometimes for the grown man to hold up his hand and shout, "Stop!" But one look at that dear little boy, so bold and manly—yet also so small, so lovable, so obviously worth protecting—and courage rises up in the man. His hand goes up, an imperious look fills his gaze, and the trains and tanks and troops of the world grind to a halt.

A man like that is ready to protect not only himself, but someone else. He's ready to be a father.

# RETURN TO PARADISE

*Who despises the day of small things?*

ZECHARIAH 4:10

If you want to go to Chicago, you buy a ticket for Chicago. But how do you gain access to the long-lost country of childhood? As it turned out, for me the answer to this question did involve a geographical journey. In my continuing pilgrimage to recover my childhood, I had to go to a town called Brockville, Ontario, located on the St. Lawrence River. Here as a child I had spent ten years, still the longest I have ever lived in one place. I'd been back to Brockville a few times, but always just passing through. I'd never seen the town through the eyes of a tender, nostalgic heart in search of secrets.

So one summer, with Karen and nine-year-old Heather in tow, I set off for the mists of the past. We hopped a plane to Toronto, rented a car, and by evening were settled in a motel room in Kingston, just an hour's drive from Brockville. I wanted to make the last leg of the journey in daylight, for this was the heart of the Thousand Islands and I knew we'd have a beautiful drive along the St. Lawrence River.

When we got up in the morning, however, it was pouring rain. I was crestfallen. So far the trip had been attended by a number of other obstacles, pressures, small disasters. A rainy day was the last straw.

Suddenly I was in desperate need of some quiet time alone to try to figure out what I was doing here. Heather was channel surfing on the TV, something that drives me bananas, so I escaped to the parking lot and sat in the car. It was 7 A.M. and the rain was pelting down. I felt small, lost, forsaken, and far, far away from anywhere.

I began to cry. I don't cry often, and when I do, it's just a few tears. But these were real sobs. Then, to my astonishment, I began to laugh. I don't know why, but something struck my funny bone and I hooted and howled. Maybe it was just the way this preposterous holiday seemed to be falling to pieces. After laughing for a while, I cried again. Then more crazy laughter, more tears, and so on.

For about half an hour I sat in the car, alternately laughing and crying in the teeming rain. This had never happened to me before. I had no idea what was going on. But I had sense enough to recognize it as the work of the Holy Spirit, and I let it happen.

By the time I returned to the motel room, I was a new man. Gone were my doldrums, there was a spring in my step and a twinkle in my eye. I recall standing in the doorway and whispering to Karen in a mischievous, conspiratorial voice, "Do you realize that no one we know in the whole world could find us right now? Nobody knows we're here!"

For some reason this struck me as the funniest thought in the whole world. While Karen regarded me askance, I laughed and laughed like a loon. I was right out of control.

Two hours later, after a good breakfast, the sun came out and we had a beautiful drive along the river into Brockville.

Later I realized that the tumult of emotions I experienced that morning was part of the high, protective wall surrounding my childhood. It's not hard to buy plane tickets, rent a car, and drive to the place called Brockville. But to get to the Brockville of my youth, I had to blast through a barrier of concrete in my heart.

Time travel is always like this. Such a journey is not undertaken rationally. Rather, one travels through clouds and mists of pure emotion. My tears and laughter were like strata of sedimentary rock laid down by season after season of the folly, mayhem, trouble, absurdity, sadness and violence of passing through adolescence into manhood. How else can one leave behind the charmed paradise of childhood and enter the self-consciously neurotic world of an adult, except by burying the former under a mountain of numb forgetfulness?

No wonder my return to Brockville was fraught with practical difficulties and with inner turmoil. The final barrier was the weeping rain, which like a last misty veil had to be lifted before the shining country of childhood could appear.

Before arriving in Brockville we stopped at a riverside park called Brown's Bay, a spot where our family had often picnicked on weekends. Though I had no particular memories of this place, I felt a mysterious softness surrounding it. I had to stop here and investigate.

I was not prepared for what I found. From the moment I stepped out of the car, I felt I had entered into paradise. My feet practically floated over the ground. The green of the grass was so pure and lovely, and the trees looked softly brushed as in an Impressionist painting. The river, the islands, and the rain-washed air, dazzlingly clear, made a scene of indescribable beauty.

I couldn't get over that I had lived in this corner of the world for ten years without ever being aware of its spectacular beauty. What I felt was far more than just a response to scenery. What astonished me was the pure, singing peace that completely melted and filled my heart. I had never known that such a feeling could be elicited by a place. I had never known that the Garden of Eden could actually be found.

Yet here it was. At least, this was as close as I'd ever come to it on this earth. I believe that day I really did crash through the gate into the paradise of my childhood. What a surprise to find that it was not haunted by ghosts and goblins and family skeletons, but rather at its heart lay something entirely happy and good.

I did meet one ghost that day: the ghost of the child I once was. I could see him, or rather sense him, so clearly in this place. I saw him diving into the water off his dad's shoulders; I saw him wrapped up in an old brown blanket when he was cold after swimming; I saw him begging to be allowed to light the barbecue with a wooden match; I saw him clumsily kicking a ball around, swinging on the swings, shouting, hollering, running like the wind, crying and being comforted.

Curiously, the child I saw was the same age as Heather. I suppose he might just as easily have been six or three. But he wasn't, he was nine. He was exactly the age I needed him to be to help me as a father to connect with my nine-year-old daughter. Up to now I had viewed this trip as a personal journey. I hadn't realized how vital it would be to have my daughter with me. But both this day and the next, Heather proved surprisingly instrumental in drawing aside the curtain that had separated me from myself as a child.

As that child appeared, I was astonished by how absolutely, perfectly lovable he was. How could I not be smitten by this chunky, zany, moody, soul-eyed tyke? Across the years this little Mike seemed to be calling to big Mike, singing out, "How about some love?" Indeed if I did not make a choice to own him and to love him—right now, today, and for the rest of my life—who would?

That day I felt like a man who suddenly discovers that years ago he fathered a child. But rather than growing up, the boy has remained a child all these years, and now he waltzes into the man's life, asking for love.

In the world of J. M. Barrie's *Peter Pan,* before you can learn to fly you have to get in touch with your "happy thought."

My happy thought is Brown's Bay.

I didn't fully understand why until the next day. After leaving there, we had continued on into Brockville where more adventures awaited. I knocked on the door of my old house on King Street East and was invited in for a tour. I walked down the tree-lined path through North Augusta Park where I used to dally on my way home from school. I visited the old railway tunnel (the first in Canada, nearly half a mile long) that a friend had dared me to walk through when I was ten. And so on.

As marvelous as it was to awaken all these memories, no other experience quite compared with the visit to Brown's Bay. Vaguely I wondered why. What was so special about that place?

The next day things took a wrong turn. I wanted to visit my former schools, but by that point Heather had had enough of traipsing around after Dad while he relived his boyhood. The thought of entering a school during summer holidays was more than she could bear. It was a hot day, and all she wanted was to return to Brown's Bay for a swim. I pleaded with her, argued; we had a family scene. Didn't she realize how important this was to me? School, after all, had been the center of my life. I'd been a top-notch student, and school held my most vivid memories.

But it was no go; Heather would not be swayed. Finally I threw in the towel, and one grumpy and rattled family headed back eight miles down the highway to Brown's Bay.

In this bedraggled state, I stepped out of the car at the riverside park and surprisingly, all over again, was overwhelmed by the clear-est, loveliest peace and joy. As we sat on the rocks of the point, swam in the pellucid water, and romped beneath the trees, gradually it came to me that the center of my life as a child in Brockville had not been school, or home, or any of the places where I met my friends. Rather, my heart's home was here, at Brown's Bay.

Why? The reason, as it dawned, stunned me. I'd left my heart at Brown's Bay because this was the place where my family had been closest.

Here, not at home, my family was most relaxed; here we laughed and played together. My dad was a businessman, always busy, always preoccupied with some deal at the office. A Saturday or Sunday afternoon at Brown's Bay was my one chance to have Dad to myself. I think my mom must have felt this way too. We all felt it. For a slice of real life, a taste of real love, we went to Brown's Bay.

The place where I thrived as a child was the place where love was. This is how Brown's Bay became for me the doorway to paradise.

On our last day in Brockville we took a boat tour through the Thousand Islands. Viewing the city from the water, I was surprised to see its skyline dominated by church spires. At least five lofty spires thrust their points into the blue like tent poles holding up a canopy of sky.

One of these spires belonged to my own boyhood church, St. Peter's Anglican. Though I had not become a Christian there, I attended regularly to sing in the boys' choir, where Sunday after Sunday I was drenched in hymns, Scripture readings, stained glass, and sacraments. At fourteen I was confirmed there, which meant having the bishop lay hands on me to be filled with the Holy Spirit. Though I was not ready to receive the Spirit, God certainly touched me. At the time I had no way of understanding the experience, but after taking my first communion at the altar rail I could hardly walk back down the aisle, so moved, shaken, gently overpowered I was.

No one I knew ever talked about such things. Many years would pass before I met even one person who could tell me the gospel. Nevertheless, as I sat in a boat on the St. Lawrence River and gazed upon the church spires of my hometown, so many precious and holy memories came streaming back to me that all at once I saw how God's grace had been following me all my life from the beginning. All along He had blessed me, watched over me, guided and protected. I saw His hand at work not only through the church, but through my family, friends, neighbors, teachers, and through the awesome natural beauty of this setting in which the zillion wild and unlikely escapades of my youth had taken place.

Before this experience, it had never occurred to me that Jesus was in the business of saving my entire life, not only the latter years but the early ones as well. I hadn't realized that His power could extend into what was already over and done, into the dark, secret, chaotic time of childhood and even into the profligate, desperately wasted years of my young adulthood. I hadn't known that redemption would be shallow and unreal for me until I let it bring light and hope, not only to my present and future, but to my past.

Reflecting on my personal history from the waterfront of Brockville, I now saw no evil in my past. Having spent decades wishing (either consciously or subconsciously) that my life had somehow been different, I now felt that everything about my upbringing had been perfect. Suddenly all I saw was goodness and mercy not merely following but chasing me down the years, until finally wrestling me into an embrace.

Gone now were the hurts, lies, resentments, and suppressed anger that had kept the door of my childhood locked. In Brockville a kind of marriage took place, a profound reunion not only between big Mike and little Mike, but between the two of us and our God. For the first time little Mike knowingly met Jesus.

# CHAPTER TEN

# GENERATIONAL HEALING

*See, I will send you the prophet Elijah*
*before that great and dreadful day of the* LORD *comes.*
*He will turn the hearts of the fathers to their children,*
*and the hearts of the children to their fathers;*
*or else I will come and strike the land with a curse.*

MALACHI 4:5-6

Since being a good adult begins with being a good child, it follows that to be a good father or mother one must first become a good son or daughter.

Most parents idealistically set out to avoid the mistakes their parents made with them. This may be possible, but not without first healing the wounds between themselves and their parents. Until this primary relationship is set right, new parents may be under the illusion that they are changing patterns of the past when really they are not. Unless the old wounds are healed, the old patterns inevitably will reappear under different guises.

Before change can move forward into the future, it must reach back to embrace the past. For children to prosper, there must be healing between the parents and the grandparents. This closes the generation gap. Think of grandparents as the roots, parents as the trunk, and children as the branches of a tree. Can leaves and fruit flourish if the roots are damaged?

Too often adult children expect their parents to change and see things their way. Ideally the older generation should bend and make sacrifices for the younger, since the onus for modeling love rests upon the more mature. However, even if elders refuse to take the initiative in building loving relationships, there remains a vital role for the young.

We're familiar with the word *father* being used as both a noun and a verb, but what about *son* or *daughter?* Shouldn't these also be verbs? Men must learn to son their fathers and their fathers-in-law, and women must learn to daughter. When a man sons a hard-hearted father, who knows whether the old man might come around? Even if he never softens, the son will be free, because love liberates the lover.

When we hear the words, "Love your enemies," does it occur to us that such love might begin with the enemies in our own families? Jesus' saying continues, "Love your enemies and pray for those who persecute you, that you may be sons of your Father in heaven" (Matthew 5:44-45).

To be good sons and daughters of our parents on earth is to be good children of our heavenly Father.

One afternoon years ago I was lying on my bed at a counseling center in Denver where I'd gone to seek help for depression. I'd attended classes, participated in a small group, and had hundred-dollar-an-hour counseling sessions.

Nothing was making sense. I wondered if I was wasting my time. With the curtains closed, I lay in a state of torpor, faintly trying to pray.

All at once something hit me. Out of the blue a new thought struck me so forcibly that I broke into sobs. For the first time in thirty years, I wept. It was a strange kind of weeping because the new thought also filled me with such excitement that I jumped off the bed and went marching around the room. From a condition of dormancy I felt suddenly on fire with life and energy.

The new thought came to me in the form of words, a sentence that I repeated over and over as I strode about the room, slapping one fist into a palm and alternately laughing and crying. The sentence was this: *"I have a good dad! I have a good dad! I do have a dad, and he's a good one!"*

A few days before this, I had sat in a lecture hall with about three hundred men. The speaker, addressing the issue of male bonding, asked how many of us had strong, loving fathers who had formed good relationships with us. At a show of hands, less than ten men in the room responded. I was not one of them.

For years I had felt alienated from my father. Though he was a decent, good-living man, he hadn't kept me from messing up my life. Consciously I thought: *If only my dad had embraced the Christian faith so he could impart some real wisdom to me.* Subconsciously I felt: *If only he had loved me more...*

If only, if only...

Now, in a flash of inspiration, I saw how wrong I'd been. The truth was that I had a good dad. If my life was messed up, it was partly because I had not accepted him as he was and received his love.

That evening I phoned my father long-distance, and we talked for over an hour. The time since my revelation had been filled with reminiscences of the many ways he had shown me his love over the years: how he'd taken me fishing, encouraged me to play baseball, arranged the best music lessons, engaged me in thoughtful after-dinner discussions, played endless games of chess and hockey and Ping-Pong, and on and on.

Suddenly I was no longer dwelling on the negative but only on the positive. It was as if a light had been snapped on in a dark room and I could see things I'd never seen before. Instead of nursing vague grudges, I was allowing precious memories to well up within me. I wanted to phone my dad to share all these thoughts with him and thank him for being such a good dad.

Can you guess what his reaction was?

Imagine: A son you hardly know anymore calls you up and gets all mushy about stuff that happened years ago. What is he—drunk or something? All his life this kid has never known the time of day. Now, all at once, he's had some big revelation...?

In short, my dad took this golden opportunity not to wallow

with me in fond reminiscence, but to give his wayward son a piece of his mind. He spilled out all the good advice he'd been trying to unload for years while his kid's skull had been too thick to hear it.

And guess what? Now this kid heard it. For once a son listened to sound advice from his father and didn't reject it. Why? Because I no longer felt threatened; I felt loved.

Reopening communication with my dad turned out to be the turning point in my depression. Once I encountered my suppressed anger and forgave my father, everything began to look different. It was like going through a tiny, secret door into an immense palace. Not only my relationship with my father, but all my relationships began to change—especially the one with my daughter. As long as I'd been a man who had not received good fathering, I could not be a good father. But now, knowing I was loved, I had love to give.

Today my dad and I are good friends. I feel completely at ease with him. It doesn't worry me that we don't share the same religious beliefs, because love overcomes all that. Forgiveness has the wonderful power of putting people on the same level and making them equals. When you perceive someone as neither above nor beneath you, you can look him in the eye and love him as yourself.

That day in Denver, one memory came back to me with particular poignancy. I was about seven and my dad had taken me fishing. We'd stayed out late and caught nothing. By the time we pulled anchor and headed for shore, darkness was falling. We were in a small boat on a strange lake, and my dad wasn't sure of the way home.

In fact, he was lost. Though he didn't say so, I knew it. Kids generally know what's happening. Probably my dad had stayed out too long for my sake, hoping I'd catch something, and now we were in a fix.

As the boat had no running lights, he got me to sit in the bow and shine the flashlight toward shore. I wasn't scared. I think he might have been, but I felt safe with him, safe because of a peculiar bond between us that arose out of the situation. We were both in the same boat, both lost, both searching.

It wasn't a father and son in that boat. It was just two human beings, two ordinary people lost together, and together finding their way home.

Unfortunately, healing between the generations does not necessarily take the form of healthy, restored relationships. One side or the other may not be ready for this. In the case of the older generation, they may be so set in their ways that they're unwilling to soften. They may be sick, senile, or in some other way unreachable. They may even be so wicked that it is better to have nothing to do with them. What then?

In all such cases there is still a balm that can infuse health into the generational roots: the healing balm of forgiveness. We forgive past generations, not because they deserve it, but because we and our children deserve to be free.

I've heard it said that life is about making peace with our family of origin and locating the family we need and deserve. Having a change of heart toward my dad brought me profound healing, not because he is such a great guy (even though he is), but because God has ordained that parents have a profound influence on their children. The Lord has set parents (even bad ones) over their children, and no child's heart can rest until it learns to obey the fifth commandment to honor one's parents. When children withhold forgiveness from parents, the shadow of the past grows ever longer, but when children forgive their parents, truly and deeply, the dark legacy of the past is cut off and fresh new growth can take place.

Similarly, parents need to forgive children. Adults in general must forgive children their callousness, their fickleness, their childish quirks, the excesses of youth. We can know whether we have forgiven children because the result will be healthy, vibrant relationships with the young.

Sadly, throughout much of society there prevails a kind of racial prejudice toward children. They're treated as second-class citizens, or not even as citizens at all but as outsiders, aliens. Most adults have no idea how to be normal and natural around children. Even when speaking to them, we tend to use a different tone of voice, a different manner.

Children make us feel frightfully insecure because we do not know how to relate to them. And fear and insecurity are the root of all prejudice. I look at that different shade of skin and I think, *This person's world is so different from mine. How can I relate? What do I say? How do I act? What could we possibly have in common?*

While children don't necessarily have a different color of skin from ours, they do have much less of it. Subconsciously we wonder: *Is it possible to be fully human with such a little amount of flesh? With such small bones and a half-sized brain? Come now, must adults really be expected to develop serious, realistic relationships with a race of beings so small and light, so out of touch with all that's important in life, so unacquainted with death and taxes?*

We deal with our uncomfortableness around children by blocking them out. For parents, especially, children can disappear off the face of the earth. They're there, you're interacting with them constantly, but you don't see them. You don't see the trees for the forest. In your desperate scheming to carve out some minuscule scrap of time for yourself, you grow blind to the peculiar reality of these odd, funny-looking beings with whom you're sharing not only your home but this planet.

I recall a youth pastor describing the day he suddenly woke up to the reality of children. One Sunday as he looked out over the congregation, his eyes happened to light upon a child. Later he reflected, "It was as if I'd never really seen a child in my life before. I'd just never realized they were there." Middle-aged at the time, this man went on to develop a dynamic ministry with kids.

I once had a similar experience, and shortly afterward I took a job as a caseworker with the Big Brothers Association. Noticing kids will change your life. Is this why many adults live as if children don't exist? Since adults are taller, it's easy to look over children's heads and not even see them. Anyone can fall into this trap at any time. Years can go by, whole decades of life, during which one never truly notices a child.

Adults who relate only to other adults grow wooden and doctrinaire in all their relationships. They are like people who live indoors without ever going outside. Children reconnect us to the real world, to the roots of our being. If you have trouble relating to children, it follows that you are a stranger to yourself and to everyone around you.

Christianity is no religion for pompous adults. It is a children's faith, a faith *of* children, *by* children, *for* children. Hang out with kids and stop taking yourself so seriously. Let children into your heart—let them disrupt your schedule, mess up your house, tussle your hair, transform your life beyond recognition—and you'll find yourself enjoying life more and filling up with love for all people. You'll find that the soul of Christianity lies not in doing good deeds, performing miracles, knowing how to pray, or going to the ends of the earth to save the lost, but in a lighthearted, easy naturalness of living that comes from being pliable, humble, young at heart.

I like finding modern equivalents for old, stuffy theological terms. Take the word *redeemed.* What if we replaced it with *rejuvenated?* This word means literally "made young again; restored to youthful vigor." The word *redemption* has a bland, traditional feel that allows us to postpone any signs of real life until after we're dead. *Rejuvenation* is a word for now. One sees a lot of redeemed folks with long, haggard faces, but when people are rejuvenated, their faces shine with life. The rejuvenated cannot wait for heaven; they're kicking up their heels and rejoicing right now.

Rejuvenation is the cure for midlife crisis. No one emerges from a midlife crisis by becoming more dutiful or sensible or respectable. The only way out is to become young again.

Being young again doesn't mean we'll suddenly have the energy of a six-year-old and spend all our time playing. No, rejuvenation just means that all ages become available to us. We grow young again by falling in love with the young. I knew a grandmother who even in her nineties was full of life and laughter and had friends of all ages. One birthday a grandchild asked her, "How old are you today, Granny?"

To which she replied, "I'm as old as the person I'm with."

Now go back and read the quote from Malachi at the head of this chapter. Malachi's prophecy contains a powerful promise for parents and children who feel estranged from one another. This promise is that the Lord Himself (if we'll let Him) "will turn the hearts of the fathers to their children, and the hearts of the children to their fathers."

This promise comforted me during the years when I couldn't seem to get the hang of being a father. Somehow my own heart needed to change; I knew that much. But Malachi's words promised that the Lord was busy changing my daughter's heart too, turning her toward me. Knowing this didn't lessen my responsibility for taking initiative as a father, but it did mean I could trust that this process was a two-way street.

The way a book ends is significant. The New Testament ends

with the words "Come, Lord Jesus"—a statement that captures the spirit of an entire two-thousand-year age throughout which the church has been awaiting her Lord's return. The Old Testament ends with Malachi's prophecy about generational healing. Not only are these the last words of the Old Testament, but they are the last words of true prophecy to be recorded until the dawn of the Christian era. During the four-hundred-year intertestamental period, the voice of the Lord fell silent. When next heard, it would take quite a different form: the cry of a baby in a manger.

As the New Testament opens, adults are being asked to turn their hearts toward a child. Parents, wise men, shepherds, prophets, priests, elders—all segments of society are called to bow the knee before the glory of God displayed in a tiny baby. Later, Jesus identified John the Baptist as "the Elijah" (Matthew 11:14) referred to by Malachi, whose ministry was to turn hearts.

Has this happened to you yet? In Jesus' day receiving the baptism of John was the necessary preparation for being a follower of Christ. Today many people are trying to be Christians without ever having had their hearts warmed toward children, or children's hearts warmed toward them.

Malachi's prophecy, besides its comforting promise, contains a stern warning: God is turning hearts, and if your heart will not be turned, the Lord "will come and strike the land with a curse." Not only will you be cursed, but the very earth under your feet will be cursed.

Why a curse on the land? Because the land represents the heritage we leave to the next generation. In an age of ecological awareness, this is no new idea; however, we must grasp that the condition of the world we leave to our children is really the condition of our own souls. It's not just our lakes and rivers that are polluted, but our hearts. People today can pour more energy into saving whales than into saving their families, but the Bible teaches a direct connection between children and the land. Children are our most endangered species.

# SELF-DEFEATING GAMES

*If anyone causes one of these little ones who believe in me to sin,*
*it would be better for him to be thrown into the sea*
*with a large millstone tied around his neck.*

MARK 9:42

When Heather was about three months old, I brought one of her screaming fits to an end by having a screaming fit myself. I must have startled the daylights out of her. Afterward, sobered and repentant, looking her straight in the eye, I spoke to her quite seriously (no baby talk) and confessed, "Heather, your father is a sinner." I explained this to her until I felt she understood. I was weary of keeping the secret that I am not God and that I am going to fail her again and again.

It was a most solemn occasion and somehow a healing one. Heather absorbed my confession more effectively than any priest or counselor. How is it that talking to a baby can be like saying a prayer to God?

By the time Heather was ten years old, I no longer talked to her directly about sin. Instead in our family we talked about playing self-defeating games. While this sounds like a euphemism, the concept had a deep effect on all of us, especially me. Ironically, to grow in childlikeness I had to get serious about giving up my games.

What are self-defeating games? A short list would include sulking, anger, lying, becoming a problem, feigning indifference, insisting on being right.

There are many others. We play self-defeating games in order to get our own way, but in the process we lose what we really want, which is intimacy with others. Such games hurt relationships because sin is never a private issue. Sin always hurts both me and someone else. Self-defeating games always result in isolation or alienation from someone we could be close to.

At heart we are relational beings, created for relationship with others. We want to answer the question, "Who am I?" but ultimately the only answer is a relational answer: I am a child of God; I am a friend of Jesus; I am my wife's husband, my daughter's father, my neighbor's neighbor.

As it turns out, I am never simply Mike Mason, for I am never truly alone. If I try to be somebody called Mike Mason when I'm with my daughter, the relationship will not work. It only works when I am her father and she is my daughter.

Since we have no true identity outside of relationships, self-seeking behavior is self-defeating. This is sin in a nutshell.

By the age of ten Heather had grown quite skilled at detecting and analyzing self-defeating games, especially in her parents.

"Dad, you're playing a self-defeating game," she'd say.

If Karen told me this, my first response would likely be, "No, I'm not." It was relatively easy to stick-handle my way through my wife's cross-examinations and justify my behavior. With Heather, however, this was not so easy. She would look at me with those frank, clear child's eyes, with that open and trusting face, and all my clever defenses came undone. What other response could I make but silence, shame, and finally humble confession?

How many precious hours Heather has redeemed for me by rescuing me from self-destructive behavior! Time and again she has performed the role of priest for me by making it safe to repent. For there is something in my daughter's face that is not in any adult face I know, something like a field of flowers or the clear surface of a lake. The faces of adults have been arranged and rearranged over years, but a child's face is her own. While it's easy to tell lies to another carefully rearranged face, it is not so easy to lie to a flower.

Isn't this why adults so strenuously avoid developing candid, reciprocal peer relationships with children? Isn't it because we do not want to be caught red-handed in our games?

Everyone has a favorite self-defeating game, and mine has been anger. At age seven Heather began telling me, "Dad, you're angry."

"NO I'M NOT!" I'd yell. "I'M ONLY TRYING TO GET YOUR ATTENTION!"

At eight Heather would say, "Dad, you're angry."

"No, I'm not," I'd quietly insist. "We're just having a discussion here."

"No, Dad, your face is angry."

At nine when Heather said, "Dad, you're angry," I'd sulkily retaliate, "Yeah, and what about you? I don't suppose *you* ever lose your temper?"

For years I got away with expressing anger to my daughter because she was too small to retaliate. After a certain point, however, she would no longer accept my anger. The moment I lost my temper she would leave the room. If I followed, shouting, she would retreat to her bedroom and slam the door in my face. If I barged in, she would lie on the bed with her fingers in her ears. Short of violence, I could do nothing. I could threaten to ground her or take away her allowance, but these were merely threats. I never followed through because I knew she was right. She was simply giving me what I was giving her: no respect. Whatever she had done wrong didn't matter anymore because I had committed the grosser sin.

By the time Heather was ten, the words "Dad, you're angry" would immediately get my attention. I'd grow quiet and just look at her. After a few moments I might say, in a small voice, "Really?"

And then she would answer, "Yeah. It hurts me when you talk like that. It wounds my spirit."

In the early stages of this process I'd think, *You feel wounded? What about all the ways you've wounded me?* But gradually even this thought faded, and I began to listen—really listen—to what my daughter was saying.

I began to let a child educate me about my anger. For I recognized, finally, that I did not know what anger was. I could not identify when I was angry, nor did I have any idea of how much anger was in me. I had to be shown and taught this by a child. By listening to my daughter over a period of years, I learned to recognize this self-defeating game and to obey the scripture that says, "Get rid of…rage and anger" (Ephesians 4:31).

Thanks to you, Heather, I'm not angry anymore. When a dispute arises, I've learned that I must be the first to soften and apologize. And the sooner the better. No matter how great the wrong may be on my daughter's side, and no matter how small I may perceive my own part to be, I must be the one to shoulder blame and to say, "I'm sorry." If Heather kicks a hole in the wall and I get angry at her, then I must go to her and say, "I'm sorry I lost my temper." I must never expect her to come crawling to me. I must crawl to her. How she responds to my initiative is up to her, but often she'll respond by owning her sin and saying, "I'm sorry."

This illustrates an essential attribute of fatherhood. Whenever anything goes wrong in our relationship, I as the father must take the initiative to set it right. And my initiative must always be self-giving, never demanding. We parents are the primary source of our children's impressions of love. When children are loved, they are good at showing love in return. But they are not good initiators—or even if they are, they shouldn't have to be. They should be loved first.

Isn't this how our Father God deals with us? When the world went wrong, He stepped in and shouldered the blame. Though He had done no wrong, on the cross He expressed His sorrow. By taking the initiative He reconciled the world to Himself. He made a way for the ancient argument to be settled.

All that remains is for us to come to the cross and say our own, "I'm sorry." No one wants to humble himself before a stern, demanding God, but when we see the overwhelming softness and humility of our Lord, how can we not respond in kind? People's hearts will never be changed by sternness, but at the sight of a crucified Savior many will turn.

Watching my infant Heather sleeping, I often marveled at how much she had changed over the past month, the past week, or even just since yesterday. And then the thought would come: *How about me? Is it possible that I too have changed so much over the past year, or even just since yesterday, that my heavenly Father looks down marveling at me?*

A sign in a church nursery quotes, "We will not all sleep, but we will all be changed" (1 Corinthians 15:51).

Parents are responsible for changing their children's diapers, but children also play a vital role in changing their parents. Dolores Leckey writes, "That parents influence children in the furthest recesses of their beings is well documented. Little has been said, however, about the young child's influence on parents, especially on their spiritual growth and development."[6]

Children change us. We don't want to change, we don't plan to, but five or ten years down the road with kids, we look back at our former life and hardly recognize ourselves anymore. The haggard housewife, the harried father of teens, the frantic wild-eyed parents of little ones: These are people caught in the terrible grip of inevitable change. You try putting your finger in the dike's hole, then your whole arm, but sooner or later you are swept away. Children are barbarians, and with barbarians on the doorstep not even the Roman Empire could stand.

In this way children make mothers and fathers of us. Whatever faults we have, whatever phoniness, whatever fears or insecurities, our children will search out these weaknesses in our armor and get under our skin. Children are wired to seek and destroy immaturity in adults. While parents help children grow up, children are busy cutting parents down to size.

Masters of the casually cruel but truthful remark, children can so easily say, "Daddy, why are you so fat?" or "Mommy's way more fun than you are." Our children aren't always right about what is wrong with us, but when a child's barb hits home, you can bet there's something that needs looking at. If a pipsqueak can cut you to the quick with a casual word, you've got some growing up to do.

Even in their silence children accuse us. When we think we are troubled about them, our worries reflect back upon us. What habits in a child drive us crazy? Behold a parable of our own faults!

In children we see writ large our own restlessness, our inner violence, our selfish callousness, our lack of discipline. If these were not our own problems, they wouldn't bother us in our kids.

To the extent that I fail to see in myself the things that trouble me in my child, I will not love her. If I want to be close to her, laugh and cry with her, and win her respect and devotion, I must get serious about giving up hidden sin. I must stop playing the self-defeating games that mar relationships. It won't be enough to live a pious, upright life free of the more obvious vices. No, like Jesus, children are looking for much more than this.

Children know instinctively that there is no difference between "big" sins and "little" sins, because all sin damages relationships. As Jesus taught, "Anyone who says to his brother...'You fool!' will be in danger of the fire of hell" (Matthew 5:22). The point about sin is not how light or how serious it is, but how readily the sinner repents and changes.

The psalmist prays, "Search me, O God, and know my heart.... See if there is any offensive way in me" (139:23-24). Children, if we let them, are an answer to this prayer. When they catch us in what we regard as "small" sins, we may assume they are exaggerating. We may go into denial and tell them they "don't understand," when really they are functioning like the Holy Spirit and searching our hearts for purity.

Children are meant to disrupt our lives and prick the bubble of our sinful pride. Who else is going to do this dirty work? Though a spouse will be happy to perform this service for us, children can sting us in a way that our peers cannot. Yet in the words of a proverb, "Wounds from a friend can be trusted" (Proverbs 27:6).

The wounds of children can be trusted because their quickness to forgive exceeds their cruelty. For any adult who truly desires to grow in love, no aid is more powerful than the child's unique combination of barbed truth telling with ready forgiveness. Like God, children show up the worst in us only to instantly forgive us for it.

# CHAPTER ELEVEN

# THE END OF CHILDHOOD

*Dear friends, now we are children of God,*
*and what we will be has not yet been made known.*

1 JOHN 3:2

Is there a definite point at which childhood changes into adolescence? Certainly there are times when a child seems to grow up almost overnight. For those who wish to become childlike, or to preserve childlikeness in their loved ones, it can be important to identify these watershed experiences. If we know when childhood ended, we'll know where to pick it up again.

Occasionally after Heather leaves for school, I like to drift into her room and sit for a while, imbibing some of the sweet fragrance of my daughter's life. Oddly, someone's belongings can seem more powerfully evocative of a person than physical presence.

One morning when Heather was eleven I was sitting alone in her room, looking around at the *Star Wars* posters, the horse show ribbons, the stuffed animals, the pile of *Brio* magazines, the school mementos. Suddenly I felt filled with emotion as the whole of her childhood seemed to pass before me, then floated away like a puff of smoke. Where had it gone? Where was my little girl?

Something had changed forever; things would never be the same. She had crossed over some mysterious border, a mist-shrouded river, from whence there was no returning. She was in new country now. The old had passed away.

The same feeling came over me that year at Heather's school Christmas concert. For seven Christmases, kindergarten through grade six, we had watched her troop onto the stage with her class to sing songs like "Santa Got a Sunburn," "Up on the Housetop," and "Happy Birthday, Baby Jesus." All the little girls would be dressed in their prettiest dresses and would look so bright, so sparkly, you couldn't take your eyes off them. It was like getting a peek into heaven at a choir of angels.

Seven years of pretty dresses. Seven years of satin, bows, lace, crinoline. And now, suddenly, it's over. This year it's slacks and a blouse.

And something else is missing too. What is it?

As I gaze across the room at my little girl among her classmates, standing there on the risers looking more self-conscious than excited—looking more as if to say, "*Must* we do this?" than "How wonderful!"—I realize what's gone.

The sparkle. The otherworldly shimmer of childhood. It's as though someone has taken an eraser and rubbed off some of the sheen from these young faces. Not all of it, but a layer. The brightest, topmost layer of sparkle is gone.

And what is left in its place?

One evening as I'm taking out the garbage I ask Heather, "Is it okay if I throw out your chenille sweater?"

This is a brand-new sweater, but with one washing it's begun to fall apart. The lint that came out of the dryer could have stuffed a pillow. That sweater is finished.

However, Heather erupts in rage at my tactless suggestion that it be thrown out. "No! No! NO NOOOOOOOO!!!"

Like a black thunderhead she bursts into a storm of tears. Over and over she screams, "That's my favorite sweater! I love that sweater! You're not throwing it away!"

There's no reasoning with her. Finally she bolts out of the house and vanishes into the forest across the way. It's nighttime, dark, and we live in a city. This is no joke; it's not safe there. Thankfully she sees something in the forest that scares her, and she comes home soon afterward. That night she has nightmares.

This is just one story, one small incident in the painfully transitional life of an adolescent. Poor, dear Heather—your chenille childhood is all washed up. The threadbare fabric won't hold together anymore. You can cry and cry and scream and stamp, but there's no bringing it back, no hanging on. Those little girl days are gone, gone forever.

I recall the moment when my own childhood passed away. I was eleven. That year my favorite uncle, who was a foreign news correspondent, gave me the best Christmas present I had ever received. It was small, heavy as lead, and wrapped in gold foil paper.

We each got to open one present on Christmas Eve, and I chose this one. It turned out to be a tooled leather box filled to the brim with foreign coins. Gold ones, silver ones, coins with holes in the middle, coins so thick you could stand them on edge. To a young boy this was the wealth of all Cathay and the Indies. Here was enough treasure that I could pick it up pirate-style in two hands and let it drip through my fingers.

But there was more than lucre in that box, for I knew that this gift had been carefully put together over time, that each piece of money had been deliberately set aside with a certain small boy in mind. Those coins couldn't have meant more to me if each one had been stamped with my own image.

Already I had a few other coins that I kept in my general treasure box along with badges and medals, rings and chains, keys, a jackknife, sundry bits of curious hardware, and finally (fatally, as it turned out) a pill bottle containing all of my baby molar teeth. Regularly I would spend time with my horde, counting the treasures like a king in exile, dreaming of the day when I would come into my kingdom, when my secret wealth would translate into public power. You see these Cub Scout badges? Really they are royal insignia. And these quaint keys? They are the keys to enormous underground vaults. And this innocent-looking jackknife? The one who wields it controls a vast army, and these odd bits of metal are tanks and planes.

In my imagination I would at times fall into the hands of the enemy and be savagely tortured. As a final warning before releasing me, they would pull out all my teeth. Fools! They did not realize that I was their ruler and that one day I would return with my vast army to annihilate them. All that would be left would be the ivory out of their mouths, which I would harvest for the building of my cities and palaces…

That bottle of baby molars was my undoing. My mother had suggested preserving them in liquid bleach to keep them sparkling white. One day when I went to inspect my treasures and pore over my destiny, I discovered that the tooth bottle had leaked, spilling corrosive bleach over the entire contents of my box.

Nothing had gone unscathed. Every precious item had been indelibly scarred. Something viler than moth or rust—Javex—had eaten my treasure for breakfast.

In my room that day I wailed like Gollum when he discovered the theft of his "Precious," the marvelous Ring. Sitting on my bed surrounded by my trove of now-worthless trinkets, I sobbed and sobbed.

Though I wept loudly for a long, long time, no one came to comfort me. Everyone in my family was in the house and I felt sure they could hear me. Why didn't they come? Were they too absorbed in mourning the loss of their own obscure treasures? The longer I cried, the more my tears became forced, arid, attention-getting. By eleven years old the deep well was running dry. But I wailed all the same, gave the siren one long, last whirl, and nobody came.

The day the Javex monster ate his way into my soul was the last time I cried as a child. I didn't shed tears again for thirty years. What good would it have done? I knew no one would come.

I don't know when Heather cried her heart out for the last time and no one came. Obviously I wasn't there to notice. But I suspect it was when Spencer died.

Heather loves horses and for years has taken riding lessons. On December 3, 1997, her favorite horse, Spencer, died. I knew at the time this was a hard blow, but I had no idea how deep the wound went until a year later as we approached the anniversary of Spencer's death.

Gradually that fall I saw Heather grow more and more unhappy, sullen, and difficult to manage. She became openly resentful, mouthy, and constantly provoked fights. Punching and kicking became her favorite method of expression. Normally fun-loving and energetic, she retreated into reading books for hours at a time—exactly as I had done at that age. As for God, He was a meany who never answered her prayers. God made Spencer die.

Parents of teenagers had warned us that adolescents go through such stages, but when you're in the middle of a stage, it doesn't feel like a stage, it feels like the end of the line. It feels like everything you have believed in, dreamed of, worked for is going down the drain.

In my own life I can pass through a dark stage and know that somehow I'll come out the other side. But when someone I love starts saying she wishes she were dead…this is hard. We thought we were losing Heather forever.

All along I've had a persistent fantasy that if Heather ever died, I would fight for her life. All alone I would go into the room with her dead body, I'd lock the door, and I'd pray. I wouldn't let anyone else in (not even Karen) because nobody I know would be mad enough to pound on heaven's door and beg God for my daughter's life, refusing to give up until He answered.

After all, she's my only child. What would I have to lose? Only my last scrap of human dignity, that's all.

Would I really do this? Would I really climb down into the grave with my daughter, take hold of her hand, and pull for all she was worth?

Until the fall of 1998, I was certain I would. But that fall I saw my little girl dying before my eyes—dying spiritually—and I did nothing.

Then it came to me, as if for the first time, that Heather had lived for years with the fear of monsters under her bed, yet I could do nothing to help her. Now, once again, there seemed to be nothing I could do.

Every once in a while in the midst of this darkness, a dim light would flash and I'd hear the words, "This is a spiritual battle. Pray for her." But prayer is the last thing anyone wants to do in a crisis. Sure, you pray, but it's not where your main energy goes. Your main energy goes into worrying, fearing, plotting, strategizing. Your imagination paints lurid scenarios and your brain works overtime, spewing out plan after plan to stave off encroaching doom.

"We'll go to a family counselor… We'll stop her riding lessons, take away her allowance… We'll just love her and never, ever get angry… We'll become firm disciplinarians and exact heavy penalties for every misdeed…"

On and on it goes. Meanwhile there's this gnat buzzing around your head, whispering, "Pray for her. She needs your prayers. I'm her Father. Give her up to Me. Trust Me and pray."

How hard this is! We don't mind praying so long as we can keep on worrying too. We Christian parents would not be caught bowing down before a pagan shrine, but night after night we kneel and worry beside our children's beds. We think we are praying, but we are not. We are worrying, and there is nothing godly, virtuous, or even practical about worry. Worry is not prayer to God, it is prayer to the person we are worried about. In effect we are praying, "Please shape up, kid, before you drive your parents crazy." We're looking to our children to bestow grace upon us. Our peace of mind depends upon their every move.

Why? Probably we feel guilty for not being good enough, not doing a good enough job when the kids were young and we had a chance. We know we're flawed, and when our children turn mean on us, deep down we believe we're just getting our rightful dues. Maybe we are. So what? Let's take our lumps and move on. Let's acknowledge our fault, ask for and accept forgiveness, and pick up our mat and walk. As long as we sit around feeling guilty, our prayers will bounce off the ceiling. Parents who believe they are bad produce children who also believe they are bad and set about proving it.

Finally, as a last resort, I let go of my guilt and shame long enough to pray for Heather. That New Year's Eve I breathed a prayer I knew was right: a clean, clear, humble, bold prayer for the darkness around my daughter to be driven back and for God's light to fill her heart.

And behold!—the Lord answered this prayer, and the new year

dawned upon a family laughing, singing, loving, even praying together. The crisis, it seemed, was over, and we emerged into the sunlight of peace.

As it turned out, the sun shone for only a few days, and then it was time to pray again. But this time I knew what to do. I knew not only how to pray but how to believe, and how to believe not only in God but in my daughter.

I don't mean to suggest that prayer is the pat answer for every problem between children and adults. If there's something we won't do that is staring us in the face—such as loving our child unconditionally—then prayer won't get us anywhere. It's no good having faith in God if we don't also have faith in our child. If a child seems so far gone that you cannot have faith, then at least have hope. Hope is what happens when, in the midst of over-whelming darkness, you take one small step toward the light.

Kids need to be believed in. They need someone to look up to them, not down. One trap adults fall into is that of placing themselves above children. Greater size and height, longer years and wider experience all conspire to produce an illusion of superiority. But the truth is that in the kingdom of God all people are equal. When Paul wrote, "There is neither Jew nor Greek, slave nor free, male nor female" (Galatians 3:28), he might have added, "neither child nor adult."

When a mother holds her baby, she is not thinking about being more mature, about how much more she knows, how advanced in moral understanding she is. No, full of pure love she marvels at her infant, basking in a wondrous bond of unity.

What a shame when parents lose touch with this bond as their children grow older. Kids get too big to cuddle, they start shooting off their mouths, and suddenly we wonder why they do not recognize our superiority. Isn't it perfectly obvious that we know better than they do? Why won't they listen to us?

Such injured pride stems not from moral superiority but from its opposite. Children give adults an inferiority complex as gradually we realize that they can see right through us. We are shocked to discover that all our years of painfully acquired experience mean nothing if we cannot persuade them that we are wise. Parents are only as wise as their children think they are.

This is hard to accept, but accept it we must or else remain alienated from our kids. We ourselves began the alienation when we placed ourselves above them. We must come round to their point of view and acquire the kind of love and wisdom that adolescents can sense as authentic. We must return to the bonded wonder we felt as we held that little baby in our arms.

Parents are the custodians of childhood. The problem with children is that they do not appreciate childhood. It doesn't interest them. As they grow up, someone needs to be there to hold on to what is slipping away. Someone needs to descend into the grave of innocence and take hold of a child's hand.

# REVOLUTION!

*The LORD said to me, "Do not say, 'I am only a child.'...*
*See, today I appoint you over nations and kingdoms*
*to uproot and tear down, to destroy and overthrow,*
*to build and to plant."*

JEREMIAH 1:7,10

Adolescents are natural revolutionaries. Their mission in life is to upset the status quo. If we as adults wish to be childlike, far from resisting this revolutionary fervor, we'll cooperate with the young to help them take over the world.

Young people are, after all, an underprivileged class, one of many such classes. What is so bothersome about second-class citizens is that they always want to become first-class citizens. As much as we may try to keep this a secret, everyone knows it. We know it and they know it. The underprivileged want what we have, and this makes the privileged feel awkward, guilty, pressured.

Even if we're kindhearted souls who would like to right this imbalance, often we don't know how. Occasionally we'll toss a coin to a panhandler, but mostly we walk on by. The whole situation of class injustice is so complex that we don't know where to begin to correct it. Why even try? It's easier just to leave things as they are.

The way things are is the status quo, and there is no greater threat to the status quo than adolescents. The work of the young in society is to start a new world. This is their proper role and calling. Through each generation God breathes on the earth to renew it, and so the young are destined to supplant the old order. No one else can do this vital work as well as the young. No one else has the necessary freshness. Even the most free-thinking and young-at-heart adult cannot match the radical exuberance of an adolescent.

Children are born to break molds. This is essentially why a new life comes into the world. Before this birth all the billions of humanity in all their variety and uniqueness were still not enough to express the full glory of life as God intended it. Man is a mold maker, but God is a mold breaker, a Maker of persons. He's in the business of reality: free, full-fledged, larger-than-life.

Too many adults are in the business of illusion. Like wild creatures, children refuse to conform to the tidy, domestic idyll we hold fixed in our imagination. The pretty fantasy must go. Make way for unruly authenticity! Make way for revolution!

All great children's literature is revolutionary, capitalizing not only on the new-world zeal of children, but on their innate superiority. Children's literature takes for granted a certain warfare between children and adults, in which children are natural heroes—clever, courageous, intuitive, resourceful—while adults are dull, stodgy, overbearing.

This is the secret that makes children's literature work. It carries an underlying assumption that children hold the key to life. As for adults, they are too busy dying. Countless children's books contain no adult characters at all. In many others (*The Secret Garden*, for example) every adult is spiritually dead. Occasionally one meets an older character (such as the professor in the Chronicles of Narnia) who is sympathetic to, or even aids, the children's cause. But even in these cases the grownups remain in the background while children are the real movers and shakers. They are the detectives, the adventurers, the wily strategists, the warriors.

The world desperately needs to hear this message that the great secrets of life remain closed to all but the childlike. However much power big people may seem to hold, ultimate power is in the hands of the little.

The scene of Jesus chasing the moneychangers out of the temple is a familiar one, but have you ever noticed what follows in the wake of this violent outburst?

According to Matthew, immediately after this Jesus began healing people and there were "children shouting in the temple area, 'Hosanna to the Son of David'" (21:15). When the Pharisees expressed indignation, Jesus quoted to them Psalm 8:2: "From the lips of children and infants you have ordained praise" (Matthew 21:16).

How interesting. The Pharisees were furious and the children were jubilant. Young people rejoiced to see the moneychangers driven out and the healings that followed. But all the Pharisees saw was chaos, not just the disorder of overturned tables but the more profound disorder of children spontaneously praising in the temple.

How do you react to this scene? Does your heart join with the young people in sending up cheers? Or do you find Jesus' actions strange and unnerving? Do you wonder: Would He really behave this way?

Maybe you're afraid He might behave this way with you. Or maybe you wish He would. Wouldn't it be something if the Lord of Glory came storming into your temple to overturn all the tables of ungodliness, sweep you clean once and for all, and leave your heart pure and fresh and full of praise? Don't you long for Him to set free the child in you to rejoice and to shout hosannas all day long? Isn't this what you signed up for when you became a Christian? Or are you still trying to take the long way around into the kingdom?

We do not know the age of the children who spontaneously praised Jesus in the temple. They might have been any age from tots to young teens. The revolutionary spirit, while most keenly expressed in adolescence, lives in all children because they see the world differently. To them it *is* a different world. They cannot help but reform it according to their own vision. Because they are acting more than reacting, they may not even see what they are doing as reform. They are simply being themselves.

Is this so surprising? If you in middle age were to move into a house recently vacated by an elderly couple, wouldn't you redecorate? Away with those stained and faded carpets and that grimy old wallpaper. Let's have some bright new colors! This is all the young are doing: letting in some light—light they cannot help but see because it fills their vision.

Imagine you are about to go into battle and you are given a choice between two swords. Though both swords appear identical, as you test the first blade, you find it blunt as a butter knife. You can run your finger all along it without harm. But the moment you touch the blade of the second sword, your blood spurts as if it can hardly wait to get out of your veins.

Tell me: Which sword will you take into battle?

This is how adolescents view life. Their world is a practical one, hard, bright, keen, tactile. Things to which we have grown blind are to them as clear as day. In their relative powerlessness, they know that to face life successfully they must have an edge that really cuts.

Most adults, sadly, present to the young a very dull sword. Adolescents know that with such a sword they could hardly open a letter, let alone lop off the heads of the demons who stalk their life.

Children do not need adults to be perfect, but they do need them to be honest and real. The young are quite forgiving of those who honestly admit their failings, but for hypocrites they have no mercy. In this they are just like Jesus.

Young people are our harshest judges, ruthlessly scrutinizing our lives to see whether what we do lines up with what we say. We want them to accept us the way adults do, overlooking our little hypocrisies. Such acceptance is shallow, yet it's what we're used to in the adult world. It is right for the young to stand against this. They are looking for "truth in the inner parts" (Psalm 51:6), and to the extent that they do not find this, they will reject us.

Ever since Augustine much of Western Christianity has been built upon rational, propositional truth. But children have little use for carefully reasoned logic. They sense that truth by nature is not propositional, it is alive. It gains its life from the inner life of the one who speaks it. The same truth in the mouth of a phony is no longer true. To children this hard fact is perfectly obvious. They want living truth. Offering children rational truth instead of the real thing is like trying to pay off the Mafia with play money.

In the face of hypocrisy, adults tend to be polite and compromising. We know that ruffling the feathers of others only exposes our own lies. But children, though they can certainly tell lies, are not yet living lies. On the contrary, they love the truth; they are starving for truth, desperate for it. They will even lie and steal to get it. When adults lie and steal it is because they have given up on truth, but children are bad because they are desperate to know truth.

As children turn into adults, most of them will give up on the search for truth, but as children they do not give up. They keep hoping, keep searching, keep longing. If only someone will show the truth to children at a young age, they are easily molded. At a mere touch of the right key, their hearts open magically.

Not only do children love truth, but each new generation has access to greater truth than its predecessor, and each generation has greater gifts. Godly parents should expect their children not only to surpass their own righteousness, but to do so in unusual and surprising ways.

How sad that many Christian parents do not have this hope, but instead expect their offspring to be cut from the same cloth. Yet if children follow dutifully in their parents' footsteps, how will new trails be blazed? Even Jesus was able to do more than His Father had accomplished, and He promised that we too would do "greater things" than He (John 14:12).

Children are meant to be the glory of their parents. That is, they are meant to embody and live out their parents' unfulfilled, often unacknowledged, dreams. For "God had planned something better for us so that only together with us would they [i.e., past generations] be made perfect" (Hebrews 11:40).

When parents truly love their children, they are not threatened by their children's reforming zeal. Good parents know this is the way of the world. Indeed such parents will delight in their children's revolutionary ways. Even if the young show no appreciation at all for tradition, wise parents know this cannot last. Healthy parents breed healthy children, children who one day will grow up to appreciate that all they have done has been accomplished by standing on their parents' shoulders.

The time of this realization cannot be hurried; revolution must have its day. Nor should parents stand smugly aside saying, "One day my children will appreciate me." No, for if the work of youth is to begin the world anew, the work of the old is to die gracefully.

"Unless a kernel of wheat falls to the ground and dies, it remains only a single seed. But if it dies, it produces many seeds" (John 12:24).

It is right for children to increase while their elders decrease. If we do not decrease and die well, with grace and skill and dignity, then the soil in our children's garden will not be rich enough for a new world to germinate.

# CHAPTER TWELVE

# THE HIDDEN YEARS

*When he was twelve years old, they went up to the Feast,*
*according to the custom. After the Feast was over,*
*while his parents were returning home,*
*the boy Jesus stayed behind in Jerusalem,*
*but they were unaware of it.*

LUKE 2:42-43

The one story we have from Jesus' adolescence concerns a time when He gave grief to His parents. If I thought I was having problems with my twelve-year-old, Jesus' parents apparently had similar problems with theirs.

Probably this famous incident from Jesus' youth was no isolated case of disturbing behavior. True, after His parents had worried themselves sick, the Messiah did return home and "was obedient to them" (Luke 2:51). But the tone of His remarks on that occasion suggests that His adolescence must have had its share of trying times. "Why were you searching for me?" He asks with that infuriatingly cool teenage insouciance. "Didn't you know I had to be in my Father's house?" (2:49).

Well, actually, Son, this is the last place we dreamed of looking for you, and now our hair is all gone from tearing it out…

Jesus' three-day disappearance at twelve foreshadows an even more distressing three-day disappearance some two decades later: the one between Good Friday and Easter. And there were other disappearances too. The prophet Simeon warned Mary that "a sword will pierce your own soul" (Luke 2:35), and likely this happened to the mother of Jesus not just once, on Good Friday, but time and again throughout her son's life.

Consider the occasion He was preaching to a crowd and someone told Him, "Your mother and brothers are outside looking for you" (Mark 3:32). How often, one wonders, did Jesus' family have to go hunting for Him?

Or how about the forty days in the wilderness? I doubt that Jesus prepared His mother for this by saying, "Don't worry, Mom, I'll be back in a month or so."

Even at twelve Jesus must have struggled with the need to parent His parents, to teach them who He was. All our lives we teach others how to treat us, but this work begins in earnest in adolescence. This is when we start fighting for our rights—not blindly as a young child does, but self-consciously, systematically. For Jesus it was a fine line to walk between the submission He owed His parents and the burgeoning self-discovery that was already driving Him apart from conventional society.

His question, "Didn't you know I had to be in my Father's house?" is reminiscent of the words of God Himself in Isaiah 40:21:

Do you not know?

Have you not heard?

Has it not been told you from the beginning?

Have you not understood since the earth was founded?

Ever notice how teenagers like to talk this way? "Dad, don't you understand…?" "Mom, can't you get it through your thick skull…?" At some point every adolescent is driven to rise up and cry exasperatedly to his parents, "Didn't you know…?" Didn't you know I had to be somewhere else, obeying other instincts, doing what I must do? Do you not understand that I *must* be true to myself and pursue my deepest urges?

To which the parents respond, "Yes, dear, that is fine, so long as you also clean up your room, get to bed at a decent time, lay off the junk food," and so on.

Sorry, parents; you lose. When you're riding the tail of a tornado, don't be surprised to get left in the dust. Both God and teenagers share a view of things that doesn't quite square with the adult world. To them certain truths are self-evident, as plain as plain, yet no one else seems to get it. This can be a source of frustration, of rage, of apoplectic incomprehension. It is also a crucible for the formation of visionaries, poets, freedom fighters, and everyone who will ever make a difference in our world.

The incandescent monomania of adolescence is not wrong, it is simply immature, unformed. Those who in later life lose touch with this teenage intensity may lead nice, satisfactory lives, but they will not lead anyone else into truth. Only those who preserve the fire of youth and learn to master it, succumbing to the status quo only in the manner of spies working behind enemy lines—these ones will leave footprints on the world's beach that the wind and waves will not erase.

The many years of Jesus' life that are not recorded in Scripture are often called "the hidden years." During this time was He, like all adolescents, hidden even from Himself? In this period between childhood and full adulthood, everyone disappears. More than at any other stage of life we ourselves do not know what is going on inside. Because we do not know ourselves, we cannot reveal ourselves to anyone else.

It would be a great help to the human race if more adults could remember what it is like to be an adolescent. One forgets how difficult it is to be transformed, largely against one's will, into a seemingly different person, and to have this happen with little real assistance from family, society, or even from one's peers who are experiencing the same thing.

How the Son of God as a teenager must have wrestled with who He was! What perplexing situations He must have faced, and how He must have longed to be either God or man but not both! Anything but this terrible pulling in two radically different directions.

Every teenager lives with this tension. Adolescence is the time of individuation, of hammering out one's identity. This work has to be done in private because that is what individuation is: learning to work things out on one's own. At no other stage of life is it appropriate to be so self-focused. In some ways this project is doomed to failure, since by nature we are not individuals but rather relational beings, discovering our identity only in relationship with others. Nevertheless adolescence is the proper time for pushing individuality to its limits.

Not everyone completes this work as a teenager; some postpone graduation from adolescence until later years. What then, besides hormones, provokes this period of radical flux?

Probably it is the questioning of fundamental principles. Adolescence begins when evaluation takes the place of ingestion. Before this time children, by and large, swallow the view of the world they are taught. But the adolescent discovers that the mind is capable of evaluating, of accepting this and rejecting that. At a certain point you look around at the world and you smell a rat, your stomach turns, you start to retch. This is adolescence.

After a few years you get tired of vomiting and you learn to keep your food down. Welcome to adulthood.

Therefore don't argue with adolescents. Don't even try to reason with them, you'll lose every time. Prove them wrong at one point and they'll instantly sprout five more arguments to confound you. You have no hope of beating them at this game because the logic of the adolescent mind is internal and exclusive. It is deliberately constructed to alienate adults.

How do you connect with someone who is leading a hidden life, whose life is "hidden with Christ in God" (Colossians 3:3)?

Not with stern discipline or angry power struggles, that's for sure. It would be easier to catch the wind in your hand or nail sunlight to a board. This is when parents discover that their child is not their own but was lent from God—a God who turns out to be far stranger than anyone imagined. Get to know this Divine Stranger, this unpredictable alien whose "thoughts are not your thoughts" (Isaiah 55:8), and then you'll stand a better chance of relating to teenagers.

When Heather was twelve, she began threatening to run away from home. Although running into the woods across the street was the closest she ever came to this, she regularly voiced her belief that the world would be a better place without parents.

As her behavior became more unpredictable, more unmanageable, more wildly self-centered than ever before, it was as if the little girl I loved had disappeared behind a cloud. Not only that, but as I had to get more serious about discipline, it seemed that not only my daughter's innocence but something of my own was lost. All the fine truths I thought I'd learned about parenting went sliding away.

One cannot live with a pubescent human without being affected by the hormonal fallout. Like it or not, the members of a family are tied together. When one hurts, all hurt. In general we think of people as being separate: I'm over here in my corner and I'm doing fine, but meanwhile my daughter is over there in her corner and she's all mixed up. But this picture is all wrong. Families have no corners, we are one body. Heather's problem is my problem. The way to reach her is through contacting the same pain in myself.

The great secret of Christian parenting is that I must feel my way inside my child, into her age, until I myself am that age before God in my relationship with Him. If a pastor is pastoring a wounded congregation, shouldn't he expect to feel some of their wounding himself in order that he may also lead them to healing?

Similarly, if my daughter is twelve, part of my role as a father is to be twelve years old before the Lord on her behalf. Even if I've successfully passed through adolescence myself, I haven't passed through *hers*. I'll need to revisit this stage in order to gain, not only deeper understanding, but compassion.

Children do not learn from adults who are mature to the point of detachment. Only through personally experiencing the spiritual lessons appropriate to my child's age can I acquire the necessary humility to pass those lessons on to my child.

In practice this means that parents of teenagers should not expect to remain calmly aloof from the fears, the unreasonableness, the wild mood swings that characterize adolescence. On the contrary, God wants us to experience a measure of these very feelings—in a sense, to enter a new adolescence—in order to connect with our teens and gain wisdom for guiding them. What better way to learn what children need than by feeling their feelings with them, traveling the same terrain?

As much as I'd like to say that I took Heather's unruly adolescent behavior in stride, I didn't. Often it scared the daylights out of me. But isn't this exactly the reaction kids hope for? Kids want to frighten their parents so much that the parents will stop disciplining them, and then they can do whatever they want. Deeper than this, kids seek to alienate their parents to prove that they are not loved. Then too they will be free to do whatever they want.

Isn't this just how we behave with God? Through rebellious words and acts we try to cow Him into submission, making Him smaller than we are. We do everything we can to test His love and to alienate His affections. Why? To shake free of Him!

Threatening the relationship is our one big stick. Whenever we don't get our own way, we either cool or break off relations. Against parents this trick often works; against God it never does, but this doesn't stop us from doing it over and over.

This testing behavior is vitally important. If we fail, and if eventually it becomes clear that God really does love us so much that He is not frightened or worried about even our worst behavior, then we may actually be forced to admit that we have a God who is worth submitting to.

It works the same for parents. Every time your kids knock you down, come up loving them. After a while they'll get the message that no matter how far they run, this relationship isn't going away. You think loving your adolescent isn't easy? God isn't easy to love either. Yet it's precisely the difficulty of loving Him that keeps revealing such surprising depths and angles both to His character and to our own.

My wife once remarked to me that Heather had "brought a lot

of amusement into our lives." My immediate reaction was, "Amusement?! Isn't that rather an understatement? Try bedlam. Or how about all-out chaos?" To the controlling mind bedlam is the ultimate threat; it takes a free person to laugh at chaos. And this is exactly what the parents of adolescents must learn: to laugh not only at chaos but with it.

Is it really so strange if your teenagers have a unique ability to arouse your rage and confront you with helplessness? This is their job. If you and I, or society, or even the church was responsible to uncover the truth about us, the task wouldn't get done. It takes the interpersonal furnace of a close family to get adults unsettled enough to start living their childhoods over again. Only in this way can we encounter and overcome our deepest fears in their original form and so enter as little children into the kingdom of heaven.

Thanks to children, we all have the chance of growing younger every day.

# JOYFUL SPIRIT

*Arrayed in holy majesty,*
*from the womb of the dawn*
*your young men will come to you like the dew.*

PSALM 110:3

This book has a happy ending. The past year of Heather's life, the year during which I've been shaping this book into its final form, has been one full of joy both for her as an individual and for us as a family. Just as in her twelfth year Heather seemed to cross over a river, leaving her childhood on the far shore, so in the middle of her thirteenth year I watched her cross a line from shadow into light.

Quite suddenly, in the summer of 1999, the dark struggles of early adolescence, the tantrums and the meltdowns, the hard indifference and the angry defiance were shed like a cocoon, and my daughter's personality emerged into the sunshine. From that point on, day after day she has grown more cheerful and bright, strong and resilient, loving and respectful and appreciative, confident of who she is, easy to live with, a joy to be around.

Is this how it will always be? I'm not banking on it. With seven teenage years ahead of her, I'd be a fool to say we've got it made. But I do sense that Heather has made her adolescent transition well and that now we are seeing her true person, the true young woman. I trust that whatever blind alleys she may wander down as a teenager, she will eventually and always return to the person we are seeing right now.

Indeed I believe this confident, joyful young woman stands to become more and more confident and joyful. Her very name, Heather, besides being the name of a flower, means "joyful spirit." The little girl we lived with for twelve years was the bud; now we're seeing the emergence of the full flower.

Among the many factors that have contributed to this transformation, perhaps the primary one was a church prayer retreat we attended. At first Karen and I weren't sure what to do with Heather that weekend. She had never been keen on prayer and we felt the event would be boring for her. However, attracted by the idea that we'd be staying in a cabin beside the ocean, she assured us she'd be fine. While we prayed, she could roam the grounds, explore, play, read.

As the weekend progressed, however, she seemed drawn to what was happening. The focus of the retreat was the Holy Spirit. On Saturday afternoon a long period was devoted to praying for one another, asking the Spirit to minister to people's needs and to bestow His gifts. To our surprise, Heather hung around our small group and participated in laying on hands and praying. Afterward she went out to play basketball with some of the young people.

What a surprise to discover that there, out on the basketball court, Heather was filled with the Holy Spirit! She was changed! In the weeks and months since then it has been abundantly clear that this change in her was real, deep, remarkable and lasting.

What happened? Here is Heather's own report:

For as long as I can remember I've had a habit of talking to myself. I'm always saying things like, "Don't be scared, Heather; that's stupid." Or, "You can't change this, so just live with it." And so on.

Well, that weekend it suddenly dawned on me that prayer doesn't mean putting on some phony voice. Really it's no different from talking to myself. Only instead of just talking to myself, I talk to God too. What I mean is, I'll throw in little asides like, "You know how this is, God?" or, "You were on earth once; You know what I mean."

To me this was such an interesting new thought. But it didn't come when I was inside praying with everyone. I felt like God was telling me something then, but it wasn't clear until I went outside to play basketball, which I love. Then suddenly I went, "Whoa! So that's all you want me to do, God? Just talk to You like I talk to myself or my friends? Hey, that's easy!"

This made me feel so free, so happy, so powerful. Something new came into me. I suppose it's like what happens when a girl gets a boyfriend who really cares for her—she has a whole different air about her, she's suddenly so complete and confident. That's how I felt, realizing God is so close. And I guess I've been different ever since.

Jesus wants us to become like little children. But what does this mean in practice? What does it look like, at thirty or forty or fifty years of age, to be childlike in spirit? Throughout the writing of this book I've pondered this question. Words like *little, natural, spontaneous, trusting, teachable, spunky*—even *wild and crazy*—have come to mind. Yet no one word seems to capture fully Jesus' meaning. No doubt this is why, rather than attempting to describe what He meant, Jesus simply pointed to a child.

Nevertheless, for a biblical description of childlike qualities, perhaps we could do no better than the Beatitudes of Matthew 5: "Blessed are the poor in spirit…the meek…those who hunger and thirst…the merciful…the pure in heart…."

One day, looking through the window of these familiar yet radiant words, I felt I arrived at a surprising answer to the question of what it means to be childlike in spirit. My insight was this: *Childlikeness is discovered by moving out of one's strength into the area of one's greatest weakness.*

This means the journey will be different for everyone. A domineering person must discover meekness, and a complacent person must learn to hunger and thirst. For the lively extrovert, childlikeness may be found in mourning, while for the duty-bound person who is always serving others, being childlike may look like wasting time on oneself in poverty of spirit.

For each person the mystery of childlikeness lies in the last place one would think of looking, the place one habitually avoids, the area of greatest weakness. In this way the game is fair for everyone. No one has a head start in this race, no one personality type has a corner on childlike faith.

When Karen and I were first married, a wise man told us that if our marriage was to prosper, it would happen by both partners growing in the direction of their greatest weakness, toward the other's strength. That is, I must become more like Karen and she must become more like me. Over the course of nearly two decades of marriage, this has indeed happened.

I believe this same principle holds true between parents and their children. In ways they may not even recognize until late in life, children do become like their parents. This much is inevitable. The real question is: Will parents become like their children? Will adults submit to this indignity? Will big people, in all their pride and strength, discover the goodness in little people and allow themselves to be overpowered by it? Will the old discover the fountain of youth?

I have. I've discovered it in my daughter Heather. After years of blind resistance, I'm finally submitting—joyfully—to becoming like her. Indeed in my own quest to be young in spirit, there is one word which now sums up for me the essence of childlikeness: *JOY!*

Somewhere amidst the rough and tumble of the world's fray, I lost the childlike capacity for joy. But now I'm reclaiming it. Now I am turning into the namesake of my Heather, a joyful spirit. I'm becoming like her.

To grasp how astounding is this transformation, you must understand that I have not been a happy person by nature. I've spent most of my life in a state of mild depression. I'm a writer, an artist, a moody sort. I came to faith in God through Alcoholics Anonymous, and while I have not had a drink in over twenty years, I still have an addictive personality, riddled with obsessions. Even after I'd been a Christian for several years, I went through a long and serious depression. A tendency to gloom has dogged my every step.

But listen: I have now moved so far into the sunny country of happiness that the next book I write will be on the subject of joy. Something amazing has happened to me, something so radical that it feels like a change in character. Yet really I've just returned to my roots. The quality that has most been missing from my adult life, I've been surprised to rediscover in my own childhood.

By becoming more like my daughter, I've become more like myself. I don't mean I was always wonderfully happy as a child, but my little boy had a wild, zany exuberance that I've begun to recapture. My child got more fun out of a cardboard box than my adult could squeeze out of a million dollars. The truth is that I am not only *becoming* a joyful man, I *am* a joyful man. I just haven't known about it for forty years!

What about you? What is your key to childlikeness? How would you look if you changed, truly and deeply, by becoming more yourself?

If you're a heady intellectual, becoming childlike might mean getting in touch with your heart, lightening up, learning to play and to feel emotion. If you're a solitary introvert, your fountain of youth may be found in fellowship with others. Or maybe for you the secret lies in taking time to sit still, becoming quieter and more reflective. Reading books. Daydreaming. Painting. Being vulnerable. Learning to cry. Traveling a thousand miles to invite your estranged brother or sister to come out and play.

What is it? What seems to be missing from your carefully constructed adult persona? What do you want for yourself so badly you can taste it—but you gave up on it long ago? What is missing and why do you miss it so? Is it possible you miss it because it was once there, a rightful part of you, and you let it go?

Everything we need in life was once freely given to us. We cannot be complete adults without returning to the mystery of childhood. To become childlike involves such a profound change that it may seem we must turn into different people, when really we are just coming home to ourselves.

Anyone who has read the Harry Potter books will have encountered the "Mirror of Erised." *Erised* is *desire* spelled backward. Look into this mirror and you'll see, not your physical reflection, but the reflection of your deepest desire. A miser, for example, might see himself sitting atop a pile of gold. A plain Jane might see herself winning a beauty pageant.

What about a happy person? What would I see if I were entirely happy? "The happiest man on earth," writes author J. K. Rowling, "would be able to use the Mirror of Erised like a normal mirror, that is, he would look into it and see himself exactly as he is."[7]

I don't suppose I can claim to be the happiest man on earth. But in my journey into childlikeness I do feel like the man in Jesus' parable who found a hidden treasure in a field "and then in his joy went and sold all he had and bought that field" (Matthew 13:44). In joy I've stumbled across what is probably the best kept secret of Christianity. Why aren't more Christians happy? Why is real joy so rare among us? Isn't it because we regard happiness dubiously and haven't deeply accepted that our amazing Father really wants us to be outrageously, joyously ourselves?

Becoming a childlike believer in joy has made a changed man of me, but I take no credit for this change. I owe it all to you, Heather, and to You, Jesus. You've done a good job, little daughter, of reconnecting your old man to his childhood. And to You, Lord, I say bravo for giving me exactly the right daughter to call out the little child in me.

The photograph on the back cover of this book was taken on the beach at Coronado Island in San Diego. We'd had a long day, our plans had gone awry, and I was not in the best of moods. We arrived at the beach just as the sun was setting and a magical pink opalescence suffused the air. The tide was coming in, and the whole world seemed charged with the roaring effervescence of huge waves climbing effortlessly up the ancient, inscrutable ladder of sand.

The moment Heather arrived on this scene she couldn't get her shoes off quickly enough. She was on holy ground! She ran into those waves just as if she were a Labrador retriever and her master had thrown her a stick to fetch.

"Heather!" her mother called after her. "Those are your only dry clothes! Don't get them wet!"

As for me, I was right on Heather's heels. This was too good to miss. Together we plunged into the thick of the action, wading out knee-deep and then standing there like little Davids against Goliaths, daring the waves to drench us. At the approach of a really big one we'd turn tail and run, jumping and bounding as if chased by clouds of hornets, laughing and shrieking with glee and all the happier because our only dry clothes were getting soaked.

Without Heather I wouldn't have done this. Without her I'd have gone to bed that night still nursing my grudge against the cruel vagaries of existence. Instead, I have a moment of outrageousness to cherish. I have a time to remember of being fully and joyously alive, a time when the lid came off the top of my head and my soul brushed the sky, when my laughter was louder and grander than the very roar of the ocean.

I'm not exaggerating. You can see all this for yourself in the photograph. You can see my joyous childlikeness.

And what about Karen? Standing apart with her camera, what does she remember of that day?

Karen felt left out. Whatever she was feeling, all the beautiful sunsets, all the children, all the waves on all the beaches in the world couldn't change it.

She doesn't mind me writing this, because just as often I've been the stick-in-the-mud in our family, the odd-person-out. But that day it was Karen. In fact she still tells this story as an example of standing outside the fire of life, declining to join in the celebration.

Twenty-four hours a day, year after year, eon after eon, those waves on Coronado Beach keep crashing in. Though I'm hundreds of miles from San Diego as I write, I know those waves are still streaming forth from their inexhaustible source. Tonight as I lie down to sleep, they'll still be passionately, helplessly extolling the infinite majesty of their Creator. Whatever made me explode with childlike joy that day, nothing's changed.

Right now, all around you, the magic of life is shining, throbbing, calling out to the little child within you. Will you come out and play?

I know life is hard, but meanwhile there's a party going on. The whole earth is celebrating. The very sky is poised over your head like a royal robe about to be lowered onto your shoulders. Run to your window and see!

Why not forget about duties, pressures, dry clothes, good reasons, and all your other adult drudgeries? Why not kick off your shoes right now and join your kids on holy ground?

# *Notes*

1. T. S. Eliot, "The Dry Salvages," in *Collected Poems: 1909-1962* (London: Faber and Faber, 1963), 210.

2. Antoine de Saint Exupéry, *The Little Prince* (New York: Harcourt, Brace and World, 1943), 29.

3. Abraham Joshua Heschel, *God in Search of Man* (New York: Octagon Books, 1976), 3.

4. James M. Barrie, *Peter Pan* (New York: Grosset and Dunlap, 1965), 92.

5. George Lucas, "Star Wars Revisited," *Time* (April 26, 1999), 51.

6. Dolores Leckey, *Ordinary Way: A Family Spirituality* (New York: Crossroad, 1982), 28.

7. J. K. Rowling, *Harry Potter and the Philosopher's Stone* (London: Bloomsbury, 1997), 156.